INTERNAL
ACCOUNTING

ADVANCED PRESENTATION OF THE

CHART OF ACCOUNTS

FOR MANAGERIAL COST ACCOUNTING

By

EMANUEL F. SCHWARZ
PROFESSOR EMERITUS, PH.D.
San Francisco State University

ISBN: 0-75963-169-7

This book is printed on acid free paper.

1stBooks – rev. 06/27/01

ABOUT THE BOOK

Over the last 50 years our university professors have tried to include procedures exclusively related to Internal Accounting as a part of Financial Accounting. This development is absolutely not acceptable. In the new millennium, the American Industries need to have a new Chart of Accounts specifically developed for Internal Managerial Accounting. No more inadequate terminology as Overhead. We need to have clearly established Departmental Operating Cost Accounts. No more using Work in Process inventory description for Production Cost accounts.

You will learn here about an absolutely new approach to structure Chart of Accounts only for managerial accounting. No more mixing Financial Accounting with Internal Accounting. This new Internal Accounting System will give management information never before received.

THE INTERNAL ACCOUNTING SYSTEM

Short description prepared by Emanuel F. Schwarz, Professor Emeritus, Ph.D.
San Francisco State University, San Francisco, CA.

The definition of Cost Accounting as established in the Management Accounting Terminology booklet, is saying:

> **"It is a technique or method for determining the cost of a process...the Cost is determined by direct measurement, systematic assignment and rational allocation."**

The technique that these professionals are referring to, and the measurement, the assignment and allocation, must have a very special accounting structure. **The necessary internal procedures and transactions belong to a whole new system arrangement. A new internal Chart of Accounts.** We will NOT be able to establish a good picture of these procedures if we only use the Financial Accounting flowchart, **because the External Accounting was never meant to be Cost Accounting.**

What system would we have to build in order to comply with these needs and requirements? A new Chart of Accounts – specifically structured for the Internal Accounting, with accounts for Departments, Functional Activities, Reallocation and detailed structure for Absorption Costing.

Within Cost Accounting, or as it may be called " Internal Accounting", we have to use different approaches to questions of evaluations of production costs compared to the general views express in GAAP. The rules and regulations within the Internal Accounting must provide specific information for internal use within a company. THE NEW CHART OF ACCOUNTS will give Management information that they have NEVER received from the Financial Accounting's chart of accounts and detailed facts that will be highly important to manage their company.

In NO way we should continue within the next millennium with same accounting structure as our good University Professors have shown to their students for the last 50 years.

It is **absolutely unacceptable** that our Cost Accounting books and the large CPA companies still try to include within the Financial Accounting's Chart of Accounts procedures that belong **exclusively** within the Internal Accounting.

It is **unreasonable** that we, Professionals of accounting science, still use the term Overhead and in real life charts, use only ONE such Overhead account for ALL production departments of our company. Today we do not have any acceptable structure of the Chart of Accounts, that could be used for the important Responsibility Accounting System.

This Responsibility Accounting System must be referring to all departments of our company and not only for the production departments. We also have to reject as **unacceptable** the account called Work in Process Inventory. This term was created only because our Professors had to have some account within the Assets of our company that would fit within the group of

Inventory accounts. But this account is showing the production cost of some product and NOT the value of only the work in process that was left over in the production department to end of the last day of the month.

It is also entirely poor to say that this Work in Process is an <u>inventory account.</u> No company is controlling this Work in Process in a way as inventory should be controlled. So this expression of Work in Process Inventory is only necessary to fit Internal Accounting's production cost accounts into the frame of External Accounting.

This is an absolutely unacceptable procedure. So let us turn away from the vocabulary of Work in Process and establish a more correct term for these accounts:

Functional Activity   should be the classification of these accounts that will show management the production cost. And under this terminology we also have to control the cost of maintenance (specially the preventive maintenance) and repair. Today our Cost accounting has none such accounts.

Management will also receive information about the cost of the company's internal production. Some companies are producing their own tools, dies, etc.

In this book about Internal Accounting we are showing you how to create the Internal Chart of Accounts from the very beginning with all necessary Cost Elements. We guide you in the process of how to **allocate** the <u>Indirect Cost </u>to the different departments (Administrative, Sales, Direct Production, Indirect Production and Service) and the Direct Cost to the Production Cost accounts. The new Chart of Accounts with its special emphasis for managerial information is also perfect structured for the purpose of **reallocation** of the Service Departments Operating costs and the **absorption** of the Direct Production Departments Operating costs by the different products and activities that the company has.

In this book about Internal Accounting you will find answers to many unsolved accounting problems that you have today.

Read it and give us opportunity to serve you.

Sincerely yours,
Emanuel Schwarz
Professor Emeritus, Ph.D.
Email: IntAccEng@Aol.com

FROM EVERY POWER
THAT HOLDS THIS WORLD IN CHAINS
MAN FREES HIMSELF
WHEN SELFCONTROL HE GAINS.

Goethe

CONTENTS

PREFACE

As accounting professionals we have learned something extraordinarily new within the field of Accounting. The structure of General Accounting is very well known to us, and we are perfectly aware of how the cost-flow chart works. But to days cost-flow chart only shows transactions related to **External Accounting.**

However, accountants do not have any specific cost-flow chart which would exclusively refer to **Internal Accounting, also called Managerial Accounting.** Through the years, many professionals has tried to incorporate transactions related specifically to Internal Accounting into the frame of the External Accounting cost-flow chart. But they had to accept the fact that General Accounting has not been prepared for internal managerial transactions.

The External Accounting was never meant to be cost accounting. After several years of research, what we have developed is a more logical approach: that makes Cost Accounting independent of the General Accounting. In other words, let us separate the External Accounting from Internal Accounting.

This concept was recognized by Professor Schmalenbach (1928) in his research work as far back as 1928 in Germany .at the Stockholm School of Economics in Sweden, Professor Schwarz studied these and other research concepts developed by the Swedish Association of Metalworking Industries, published by Professor A. ter Vehn. (1957)

Professor Schwarz worked with the United Nations Industrial Development Organization, Vienna, Austria, for 10 years as consultant to governmental and private industries. During that time, Schwarz developed and extended in a more practical way the proposed new chart of accounts.

Many professionals encouraged Professor Schwarz to work on this research project that would bring these new concepts of Internal Accounting to American universities and to professionals in the field of Managerial Accounting.

We are certain that this new Internal Accounting cost-flow structure will make the study of Managerial Accounting much easier to understand, and that it will help our students and managers in their effort to understand and use effectively this field of Internal Accounting.

Emanuel F. Schwarz
Professor Emeritus, Ph.D.
San Francisco State University.

ACKNOWLEDGMENTS

The idea for this book was originally inspired by Professor A. ter Vehn from Stockholm School of Economics, Sweden. By some means, he foresaw that in a time span of 30 years, his student, Emanuel Schwarz would have the opportunity to realize this present book.

Professor Charles Horngren from Stanford University encouraged me to continue his research to bring forward a modern internal accounting structure.

Professor Thomas Johnson and Robert Kaplan gave me strong support with their book RELEVANCE LOST.

Professor William Ferrara, with all his remarks, is especially responsible that this research work was realized.

Professor Steven Mintz, Chair of the Department of Accounting, helped very much to conclude this book.

But the greatest acknowledgment is given to Professor Carl Warren. His support was an immense help.

Much hard work was invested by Don Mattison, to get my writings into readable English.

My wife gave me the necessary Colombian coffee and the spiritual support, to work through hours of creating these pages.

CHAPTER 1

INTRODUCTION TO ALL WHO SEARCH FOR PROGRESS

During the last 10 years, accounting professionals have heard much about problems linked with academic teaching of Managerial Accounting. Magazine articles and books have been written about the problems in teaching and explaining to students the accounts flowchart as it is used today. One problem lies in the fact that this flowchart refers exclusively to the Financial Accounting system and does not have a cost flow structure that specifically relates to the Internal Accounting.

This flowchart shows us accounts referring to Assets, Liabilities, and Revenues but only the Overhead group of accounts refers to the Internal Accounting.

All cost accounting books use this present accounts flowchart. They try to explain and to show to students the relationship between External (Financial) and Internal Accounting. A detailed analysis of these flowchart graphics, gives us a clear awareness of how misunderstood this association is.

The account called overhead is a good example. There are cost accounting books that suggest in their graphics that this Overhead account is part of the Assets. In this book, we will show the ways in which these terms of Overhead and Work in Process are misunderstood and misinterpreted. The basic purpose of our research project is to develop an accurate Internal Accounting flowchart and establish clear links between Overhead and Work-in-Process accounts.

Those who have studied cost accounting with graphics that are used today are now working with CPA firms, and consequently, we find that most (if not all) CPA firms recommend to their clients a Chart of Accounts just as these old graphics indicate. It is very seldom that a manufacturing firm will have a Chart of Accounts that will show some specific accounts refer- ring to Internal Accounting. These Charts of Accounts do not have Overhead accounts as part of their structure because they have detailed Expense accounts. If they also would have Overhead accounts, they would record expenses twice. This is a very important key point which we denoted in the Introduction. Professionals in the field of accounting are all very well aware that a significant difference exists between the cost flow structure that is being taught in Principles of Accounting and the cost flow that is shown in Cost Accounting books. Moreover, our research to provide more accurate Internal Accounting consistently brings forward the differences and problems that arise from this apparent conflict.

The strongest protest against this cost flow structure can be found in the book <u>RELEVANCE LOST</u>, written by Professors Thomas Johnson and Robert Kaplan 1987. These well known professors clearly state that the present accounting system is obsolete, and that something must

Emanuel Schwarz

be done to develop Internal Accounting. Professor Johnson gives the following significant statement:"... despite the enormous increase in information processing capabilities, however, most organizations still use a <u>single system</u> to generate their financial and management accounting reports."

This problem of having only a single system will be discussed in depth in this research project report. We may express the problem simply in the following way:

NOT TO DEVELOP ONLY ONE SINGLE FINANCIAL

ACCOUNTING SYSTEM, BUT CREATE WITHIN IT,

AN INTERNAL ACCOUNTING STRUCTURE.

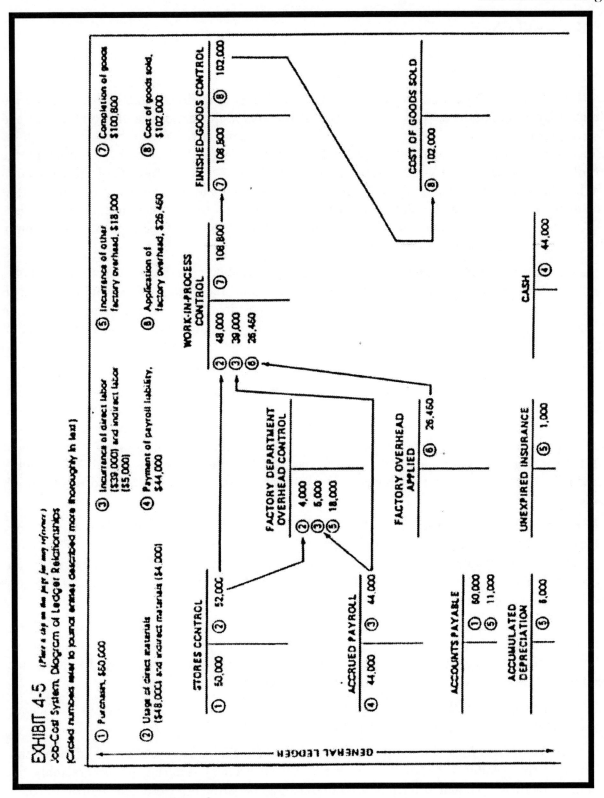

EXHIBIT 1--1: Professor C. Horngren's Cost-flow Chart.

THE CHALLENGE

Let us analyze the following three graphics which represent the most important cost-flow structures that we have in our cost books: Exhibits 1-1, 1-2, and 1-3.

Exhibit 1-1 is the classic presentation. The student is told direct materials are transferred from credit Stores to debit Work-in-Process. It is obvious in this exposition that both Stores and Work-in-Process accounts belong to the Assets of the company. Consequently, the Work-in-Process account does not correspond to the Internal Accounting, and through this structure, the whole meaning of the Work-in Process has been transformed to total amounts of the production during the month. The amount of work in process corresponds to the value of production left at the moment of closing the last day of the month. Unfortunately, this concept has totally changed: the Work-in-Process account is used as if it would be the Production Cost account of the month. Why does this misrepresentation endure?

The answer to this question is simple: Since no Internal Accounting flowchart exists today, and the flowchart refers only to the External Accounting, the account that would be used to register the production cost of the month could not be identified with the name "Production Cost." Within the Assets we just could not have an account that would refer to the production cost of the month. The accountant had to designate the name of "Work-in-Process Inventory" to this account.

It can be clearly seen now, that an accurate Chart of Accounts should not have any account called "Work-in-Process." The reason is very basic: We should not name an account referring to its ending balance. The name of an account should tell us the basic purpose of the account. And the purpose of this account is not to establish the amount of the Work-in-Process at the moment of the closing the month (normally it is a very small amount compared with the monthly production), but it is to inform management of the production cost of the period or of the job order.

Another challenging problem in Professor Horngren's graph is the following: The Factory Department Overhead Control accounts are included in the General Ledger accounts. This brings a conflict to the whole Chart of Accounts. If we include the Factory Department Overhead accounts in the General Ledger, we then have to exclude the Expense accounts from it. Because both should not appear together in the same General Ledger.

It is obvious that a significant problem exists here. In principles of accounting, we teach our students the necessity of opening expense accounts. When our students learn cost accounting, we simply exclude these expense accounts in the flowcharts. The basic problem here lies in the fact that today's flowchart has no Internal Accounting structure.

The next graph on the following page, Exhibit 1--2, is prepared by Professor E. Deakins (1987). Here we can see a mix-up of departments and Work-in-Process accounts.

The Manufacturing Overhead accounts refer to the different factory departments. Consequently, Exhibit 1-2 should have one overhead account referring to the assembly and another overhead account referring to the finishing department. Here the Work-in-Process

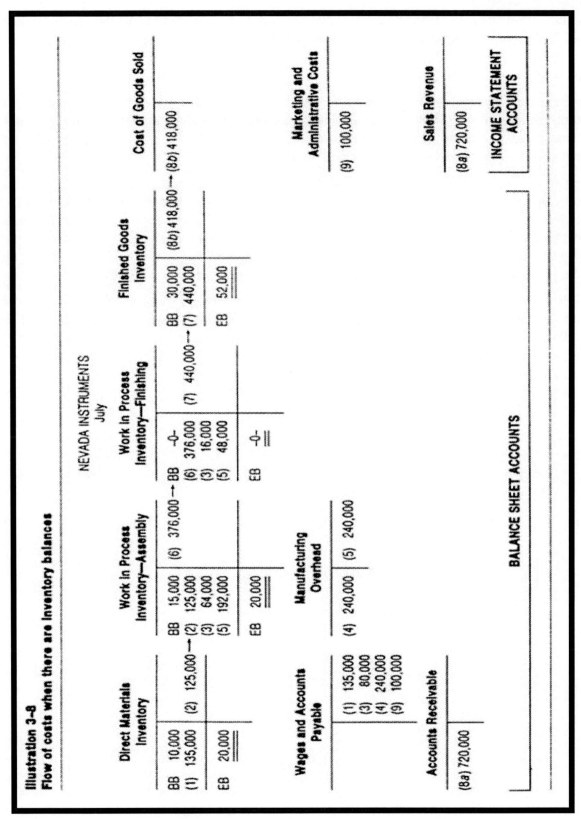

EXHIBIT 1--2: Professor E. Deakin's Cost Flow Chart

5

account (Production Cost) is attached to the department's name and not to the product's name. This factory many assemble different products which would be controlled by job orders. It is necessary to open as many Production Cost accounts as there are different products (or group of products).

Our next observation is that Exhibit 1--2 shows our students that the Manufacturing Overhead is a Balance Sheet Account, which is an incorrect statement. The mix up here arises because this flowchart of costs tries to combine internal accounts within the External Accounting, which is not an accurate or correct approach.

The third graph, Exhibit 1--3, is the most interesting one (see next page). It was prepared by Professor R. Anthony. The special, most interesting observation is that Professor Anthony is of the need to divide the flowchart into external and internal transactions. To the left, in the flowchart we can see the part of the chart that refers to the External Accounting transactions related to acquisitions; to the right, a dotted line separates the sales transactions which also belong to External Accounting. In the center are the accounts referring to Production Cost.

Professor Anthony just could not change the name of these accounts, so he still uses the Work-in-Process Inventory nomenclature. Students often become confused when they read that the Work-in-Process account is an inventory account. They receive the impression that the Work-in-Process is controlled in same way as an inventory account. That does not correspond at all to the practical reality of the facts of the situation.

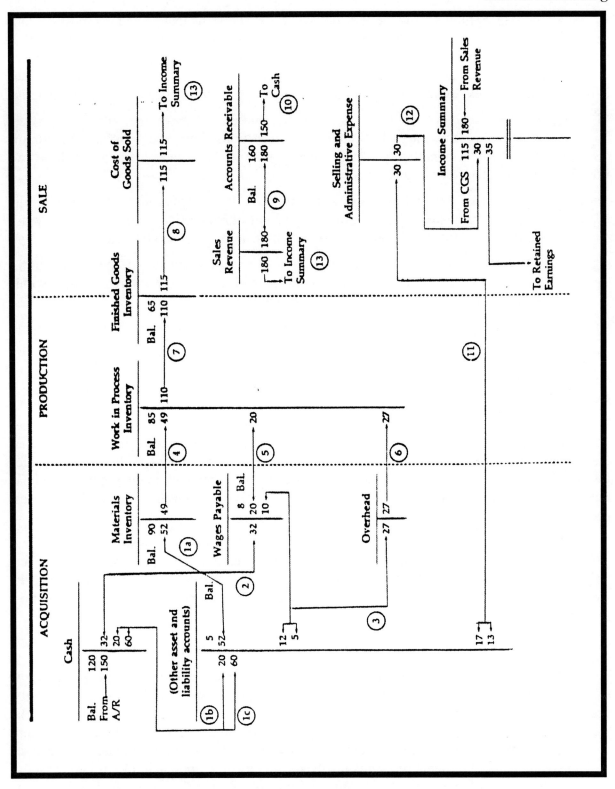

EXHIBIT 1--3: Professor R. Anthony's Cost Flow Chart.

Never the less, Exhibit 1--3 is the first flowchart that shows us that something must be done to develop an Internal Accounting structure. Naturally, such a structure would relate and reflect clearly the production cost account and other accounts that specifically describe the internal transactions of the company. Professor Anthony certainly has the basic idea. What must be added is that necessary breakthrough modification to separate the internal accounts from the external accounts.

This separation of the Internal Accounting transactions from the External Accounting transactions is the great opportunity that this book presents. With the separation of these two flowcharts, we gain the following basic advantages:

1. The External Accounting graph will again show the Expense accounts as is generally taught in principles of accounting. Further in our report, we will analyze how this Expense account should be designated with the term: EXPENDITURE.

2. The Internal Accounting graph will be a totally new presentation of the concept of the cost-flow within a company. This concept will create new awareness first within current students and then within management.

3. The Internal structure will open a totally new relevance for accounting transactions. These recordings will be built upon the needs of managerial requirements rather than based artificially upon GAAP regulations.

GAINED RELEVANCE.

For many years, accountants had to work manually with the present accounting system. They were overloaded with daily routine work and had no time to dedicate their attention to new managerial concepts. For these busy accountants, it was just about impossible to prepare detailed information about responsibility centers and production cost. They had no other choice (and had received no other education) but to work with one Overhead account and one Work-in-Process account.

With the introduction of computers with high speed processing capacities, accountants gained a completely new opportunity to prepare detailed reports. It is now both necessary and possible to develop a new cost-flow structure that not only accurately represents new Financial Accounting (the External Accounting), but which also has an Internal Accounting cost-flow structure.

THIS NEW STRUCTURE WILL BE THE GAINED RELEVANCE.

In all honesty, we should probably acknowledge that many current university accounting students are not getting a clear picture of Internal Accounting cost-flow. We still, unfortunately, use the same graphic structures that were created some 50 years ago when only Financial Accounting was considered. Professors who wrote cost accounting books then used these graphs and tried to develop some internal costs within this External Accounting frame. As discussed previously, there are significant problems involved using this old approach. In this context let us consider the following comments by Professor Thomas Johnson "... One might wonder why university researchers failed to note the growing obsolescence of organizations' management accounting systems and did not play a more active or more stimulate role to improve the art of management accounting system design."

And, it might be added, especially when in Europe internal accounting procedures and structures had already been developed.

The purpose of this book also includes laying the ground work for a clear terminology within the teaching of cost accounting.

Let us establish the difference between the present and the proposed cost-flow arrangement. The charts in Exhibit 1--4 clearly shows the basic structural distinctions.

(Turn to next page.)

The analysis and descriptions we developed on previous pages, will help us to understand the enormous difference:

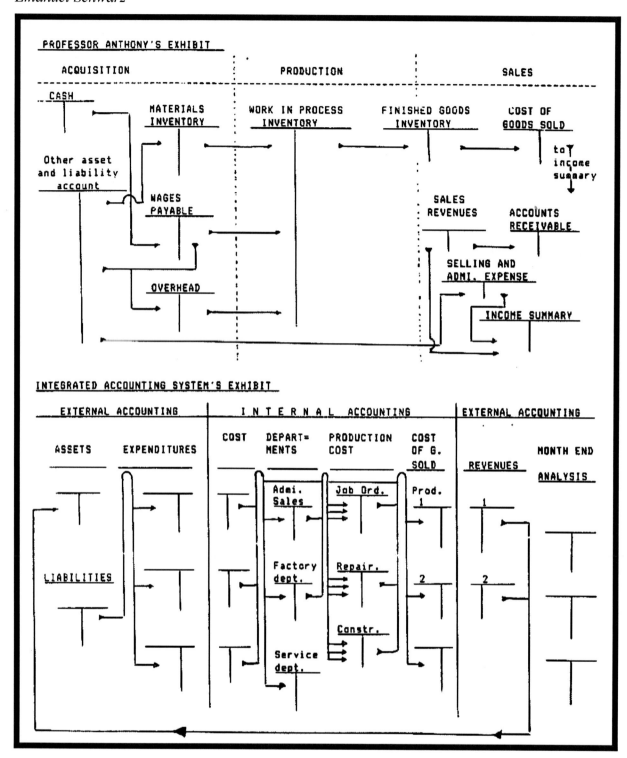

EXHIBIT 1--4: Professor Anthony's (top) and the proposed cost-flow structure (bottom).

The Integrated Accounting System has opened the flowchart and introduced in the center part the Internal Accounting structure. The Integrated Accounting System clearly shows more than one group of accounts. The center part, the Internal Accounting structure, shows more than just the production cost. It presents a new, more detailed concept of Managerial Accounting.

This total new arrangement has special classes of accounts which refer to various Cost Elements, to different Departments, and to a special class of accounts exclusively provided for the Production Cost accounts. It can also be seen that this Production Cost class of accounts has two new important groups of accounts related to cost of repairs and internal construction. The control of these two activities within our manufacturing companies are today misrepresented or ignored in our cost accounting books. Finally, we have a class of accounts referring to the Cost of Goods sold.

No Work-in-Process accounts are incorporated within the Internal Accounting. These WIP accounts will be registered within some group of Assets to show us the different month ending balances of the Production Cost accounts.

We recommend that the "Overhead" terminology be rejected. Like Professor Horngren, we also chose to name these accounts in accordance with the different departments within the company. With this new Integrated Accounting system, not only can accounting refer to the production and service departments, but also to all other centers, such as administrative, sales and indirect production departments.

Within the new Integrated Accounting system there is now a very important concept reflected within the cost structure: By creating the Cost Elements class of accounts, we have introduced to the Internal Accounting the MATCHING CONCEPT that is generally taught in the principles of accounting. The Internal Accounting system not only refers matching of the expenses toward the revenues, but it also incorporates the important matching concept of the costs toward the production.

Another of the many important factors in this Internal Accounting system is that we have separated the accounting transactions of the External Accounting from the Internal Accounting transactions. Consequently, there may be different dates when we finish External Accounting from the date we accomplish the Internal Accounting. This separation will also make it possible to include different Cost Elements within Internal Accounting, which currently are not acceptable because of regulations controlled by GAAP.

With this new Integrated Accounting system, principles of accounting can be taught and understood in a more realistic and practical way, and the new accounting generation will bring management a clearer, more accurate picture of the internal accounting cost-flow.

11

CHAPTER 2

DEVELOPMENT OF
THE FINANCIAL
ACCOUNTING

From the very beginning, our System of Financial Accounting had to give the user all the information needed regarding the amounts of money the company had at its disposal and how much the company owed. The Assets accounts were established and organized in such a way that the user could have the possibility of including within this class of accounts, amounts which were recorded as Assets for the actual purpose of keeping these amounts for future periods (prepaid expense), and which reduced the problem of matching cost toward revenues. This procedure of keeping expense amounts within Assets directly brings out the need for having a logical meeting of corresponding expense amounts with the amounts of revenues for a given period.

Many prepaid expense accounts have no actual value as something that a company has as an asset amount at its disposal. But the Financial Accounting authorities agreed at one time, that it would be unwise and would give an improper picture of a period's profit or loss, if in the Income Statement, a company charged as cost, amounts that logically did not correspond to or occur in this time period.

This dilemma makes clear the need to understand the requirement to identify the <u>expired</u> portion of these expenses. This expired portion is the amount which is acceptable as correct to deduct from the revenues. A calculated amount is determined that is believed to be acceptable to charge to this given time period. The most classic example of the problem of expired portion of expenses is depreciation.

For depreciation, we calculate the amount per month, per mile or per machine hour and use this amount to establish the most correct cost of goods manufactured. The entire procedure of the expired portion brings us to a key of the Internal Accounting System concept. For External Accounting (or the Financial Accounting), the expired portion system is used only once a year, usually when the Income Statement is prepared. We analyze the expenses and decide which of them must be transferred to the next fiscal period.

To establish more specifically the manufacturing cost, with more advanced thinking about Internal Accounting, the general accountant had to recognize the need for this expired portion, and consequently developed more and more prepaid expense accounts. Inevitably, in Internal Accounting where the actual need to use these expired portions is dominant, it becomes clear that the matching problem is just as important in the Internal Accounting as it is in External Accounting.

Before the teaching of Responsibility Accounting surfaced, the accountants used (and some still are using) large subsidiary ledger books with many columns to record the cash expenses. We vividly remember how we had to write down the different expenses in those specific columns. And these expenses, identified with their specific names, were part of the Owners Equity. We divided this basic account of Owners Equity into two clearly established parts which we called: Expenses and Revenues. To these Expense accounts we charged the expired portions of our cost (expenses). All our Chart of Accounts had these Expense accounts. As time passed, we recognized the need to have responsibility accounting.

Accounting professionals and professors were in a dilemma: Where in the Chart of Accounts, and consequently in our cost-flow structure, should we place these new accounts that would represent the different cost centers which we would like to control with this new responsibility accounting system? There was no other choice than to eliminate the Expense accounts in our cost-flow graphs and replace them with cost center accounts. We called these accounts Overhead.

Surely many readers of this paper will remember Professor Horngren's footnote in his Cost Accounting book (Sixth Edition, Prentice Hall, 1987), in which he says: " Why did we not call these accounts UNDERFOOT instead of Overhead?" This question now belongs to the ages.

It should be noted that in our Chart of Accounts we have not eliminated Expense accounts they remain and are still used. We introduced Overhead accounts in our Chart of Accounts only for internal use. A financial accountant ignored these accounts and did not record them either in the Income Statement or in the Balance Sheet. A financial accountant just could not have used these Overhead accounts because he would have recorded many amounts twice. There would be salaries charged to the Salary Expense account and the same amount charged to the Overhead accounts. So the problem lies in the simple fact that these Overhead accounts actually do not belong to the External (Financial) Accounting. They are, however, necessary to internal management information.

Again, we have the problem of trying to force into the External Accounting frame accounts that do not belong here. It is difficult to find a cost accounting book in university libraries that explain this problem. And many of us who are university professors know how much confusion exists in the minds of accounting students (and those who later became managers) about this Overhead account.

This one Overhead account, which is shown in all graphic cost-flow structures has also created many bad habits in manufacturing industries. The accountants use just one Overhead account for all production departments. Clearly this is inadequate and inaccurate.

The study about COST MANAGEMENT SYSTEM CMS conducted by CAMI from Arlington, Texas, has confirmed this problem of using only one absorption rate.

Service Departments should also be included within the group of Overhead accounts, and these Service Departments cost should be reallocated to the actual departments that receive the service. Graphically, it is not shown at all, and accounting students do not receive a clear idea of how to reallocate costs.

Let us now ask the following: Should Responsibility Accounting only refer to Production and Service departments? Should we not include in this system also Administrative and Sales departments? The answer is obvious. We should control all departments in our company not just the Production and Service ones. Where do we have these Administrative and Sales departments in Professor Anthony's graphic presentation? They are under the sales activities of our company graphically to the right of the whole cost-flow picture. Do both administrative and sales departments actually belong to the Sales activity? Not non-sales Administrative departments. Here again we are in difficulty because these departments have nothing to do with the Financial (External) Accounting.

Let us now analyze the Management Accounting terminology which the National Association of Accountants published as a Statements on Management Accounting No 2 on June 1, 1983:

COST = the cash required to attain an objective such as acquiring the goods used, producing a product.

EXPENSES = outflows of assets ... from producing goods. The expenses of a period can be costs associated with the period on some basis other than a direct relationship with revenues and costs that cannot be associated with any other period.

EXPENDITURE = an outlay of cash for goods.

COST ACCOUNTING = A method for determining the cost of a project, process .... This cost is determined by direct measurement, arbitrary assignment, or rational allocation.

Of course, these terms are not clearly established because they correspond to both External and to the Internal Accounting. Without any discussion, the term COST should be used within Internal Accounting. In Internal Accounting, we also use: production cost and direct cost. We also frequently use Cost of Goods Sold, which should be described as Expense of Cost of Goods Sold.

This research paper would, consequently, recommend that for Internal Accounting use only the term COST, and within External Accounting we should use Expense or Expenditure.

All accounting professionals know that accounting demands a disciplined way of working and thinking. Therefore, it is necessary to establish clear terminology. All of us who teach accounting should also use these same terms in a similar way. Unfortunately, it may take several years before the unification of terms will become a reality.

Another important analysis must be done regarding the WORK-IN-PROCESS account. When the manufacturing industry began, accountants had to create an account where the production costs could be recorded. It was not possible to open an Expense or Overhead for this purpose within the traditional Chart of Accounts. It was necessary to open an Asset Inventory account. Here again, it can be seen how an internal account was forced into the frame of External Accounting. As a consequence, all accounting literature stated: Cost accounting is to establish inventory values. This is incorrect. We should not mix External needs of inventory values with Internal needs of production cost values. Determination of production cost is the primary objective of Cost Accounting.

For an easier and clearer understanding of what we are analyzing, and the cost-flow structure that Financial Accounting uses, let us look at Exhibit 2--1, a reprint of the Exhibit 5--5 taken from the Fundamentals of Management Accounting, written by Professors Anthony, Welsch and Reece (Irwin, 1985).

This flowchart is the first one, as far as we know, that shows accounting graphics divided into three parts: The Acquisition, the Production, and the Sales. We can see clearly that the

Production section is represented with only the Work in Process Inventory account. This is insufficient for Internal Accounting. The Overhead account is still located within the Balance accounts and the Selling and Administrative Expense account is within the Sales section of this presentation of External Accounting.

Turn to next page for exhibit.

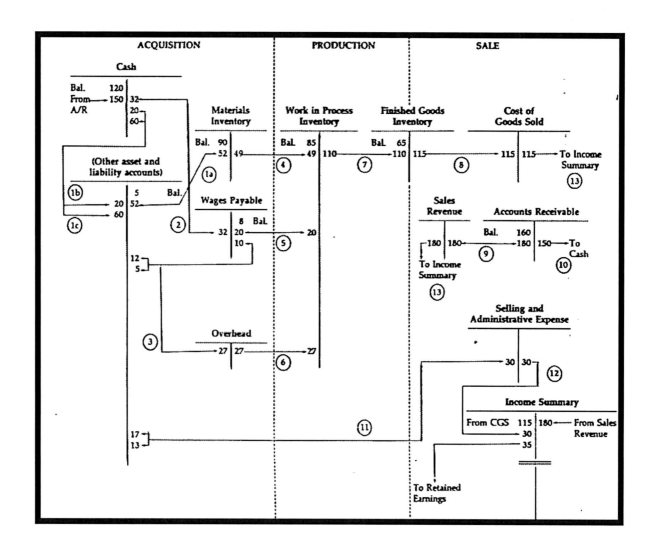

EXHIBIT 2--1: Account Flowchart.

CHAPTER 3

COST ACCOUNTING NEEDS AND NECESSITIES

To understand the whole meaning of cost accounting (Internal accounting), we indisputably have to penetrate into the theory philosophy of its structure. Let us examine the definition of Cost Accounting as established in the Management Accounting Terminology booklet, Statement Number 2, June 1, 1983 (Page 25):

" A technique or method for determining the cost of a project, process, or things used by the majority of the legal entities in a society, or specifically prescribed by an authoritative accounting group. This cost is determined by direct measurement, arbitrary assignment, or systematic and rational allocation."

The technique that these professionals are referring to, and the measurement, the assignment and allocation, must have a very special accounting structure. The necessary internal procedures and transactions belong to a whole new system

arrangement. We would not be able to establish a good picture of these procedures if we only use the Financial Accounting flowchart, because the External Accounting was never meant to be cost accounting.

What system would we have to build in order to comply with these needs and requirements? Let us look into this question in this chapter.

Within Cost Accounting, or as it may be called "Internal Accounting," we have to use different approaches to questions of evaluations of production costs compared to the general views expressed in GAAP. The rules and regulations which we must have within External Accounting (Financial) are too broad and general to be used within a managerial accounting system, which must provide specific information for internal use within a company.

External Accounting has only two important presentations which are expressed in the Income Statement and the Balance. The Income Statement is highly simplified. It is good enough for External Accounting presentation and use, but items such as Cost of Goods sold are of little use for internal purpose because they give total information of the cost of all our goods sold. Management needs to know the cost of each item sold. Internal Accounting detail should also inform management about the cost of raw material, direct labor and the absorbed amount. For External Accounting purposes, this information is unnecessary.

If we think about this concept and refer back to the Exhibit 2--1 on page 16, Chapter 2, it can be seen that the central part of this graph, which is called Production, should be broadened in such a way that it shows all the basic structure which management needs for internal planning and control. Let us refer to them as "internal users."

The central part of Exhibit 2--1 should be indicated as Internal Accounting, and here should be the classes of accounts that are of primary interest for internal users.

If we could develop accounts that are useful for internal management within this central part of the graph we would arrive at a total new concept of cost-flow structure. We would have accounts that would show management the internal flow of production cost, goods sold and services, which would be very useful.

Through our newly defined cost accounting structure, the transactions related to Internal Accounting are separated from those related to External Accounting. Now we start within Internal Accounting with amounts which would be the expired portions of Expenses that we have had in General Accounting. Next, we develop a class of accounts which refer to Responsibility accounting, that is, control of departmental operating costs.

Within this Internal Accounting system we also open a class of accounts in which we register the cost of production. This makes it possible to avoid the present terminology and account of Work-in-Process Inventory within the production section of the cost flow chart.

The inventory account would remain within the Assets of our company. Finally we are able to open a specific class of accounts that refers to the Cost of Goods sold.

Another important improvement that we could have by using an Internal Accounting system structure, is a clearer graphic presentation. This new cost-flow would help students to understand better the various transactions within Internal Accounting. It would also help managers and supervisors of factories to understand internal cost-flow and would instill in them the proper cost awareness.

In understanding the important need to open a separate Internal Accounting structure, we have to observe the following significant points:

1. Internal Accounting will have accounts that will show specific costs matching the period of accounting (month) and that are the expired portion of expenditures accrued in External Accounting.

2. Most important for teaching purposes is the possibility of showing students and managers how these costs will be allocated to the different departments or directly to the production cost accounts.

3. Within the Production Cost accounts, we now are able to have accounts for the control of maintenance, repair, and internal production.

4. With this new internal accounting structure, we are able to prepare an internal machine lease program.

5. A key concept is that we would be able to include within Internal Accounting, the Cost of Capital for some specific production. This would be a totally new concept for a modern production cost accounting.

CHAPTER 4

THE BASIC SYSTEMS TRANSACTION FLOW

In the previous chapter we came to the conclusion that we needed an Internal Accounting structure.

Let us develop this Internal Accounting structure within the flowchart with which most accountants and professors of accounting are familiar. We refer to this flowchart on page 16, Exhibit 2--1, an excellent example, which Professor Anthony has given. He indicates graphically that to the left in this exhibit are the Acquisition accounts. These accounts may also be identified as those which register the transactions related to the external world of our industry. Here we record the values the company has and those that the company owes to others. We record these transactions in our Assets and Liabilities.

To the right of this flowchart we have the Sales accounts. These accounts record the transactions with the world outside our company.

In between these two structures, we have the Production accounts. These accounts record the internal transactions of our company. Referring to these transactions, let us see if we are able to develop a new graphic chart.

Exhibit 4--1 presents a simplified model of basic business activities: purchasing, production and marketing. Turn to next page for exhibit.

The approach shown in Exhibit 4--1 depicts the company from above (a top down perspective), including the imaginary walls surrounding the company. To the left is an opening or entrance through which "external" transactions enter into the company, such as labor, services, and materials. Through this same opening, the company pays for labor, services, and materials. In and through this left segment of the company, "transactions" are conducted with the outside world; that is, payments to employees, vendors, banks, and other organizations. In this left part of the company model, the general accounting system captures total amounts using the category or term of "accruing," recording these accruals in this part of the accounting structure.

Next, only those costs that are truly associated with production and especially with the production during a specific time period (matching problem), enter through the left internal wall. This is important because an accurate and meaningful system should not record or charge accrued amounts which do not occur in, or correspond to, the specific period. Should non corresponding charges be made, they cause the cost of production to be overstated or understated. The accountant must decide how much of a specific period's accrued expenditure corresponds to the current period's production activity, or to the administrative work, or to the marketing efforts. The importance of this point, cannot be overstated.

The total amount of expenditure (i.e., the total equal to that for all external transactions) may be charged to production activities (internal transactions). However, the expenditures must be distributed over several months or years because the company may have purchased equipment or services which will be economically beneficial to the company during many months or years of activity.

At this point, and in the interest of accuracy, let us establish some terminology and definitions that will be useful. Within the External Transactions sections, we will use the term EXPENDITURE. Within the Internal Transactions, the expired portion of the expenditure, we will use the term COST. This will help us to identify these different amounts:

EXPENDITURE corresponds to transactions related to external accounting (general accounting).

COST is the expired portion of expenditures, which relates to internal cost accounting.

The central part of Exhibit 4--1 indicates that the company is dedicated to producing something; when this product is completed, it moves through the internal partition on the right. The finished product is now in the right part of the model of the company a segment referred to as "external" and which is directly related to marketing activities.

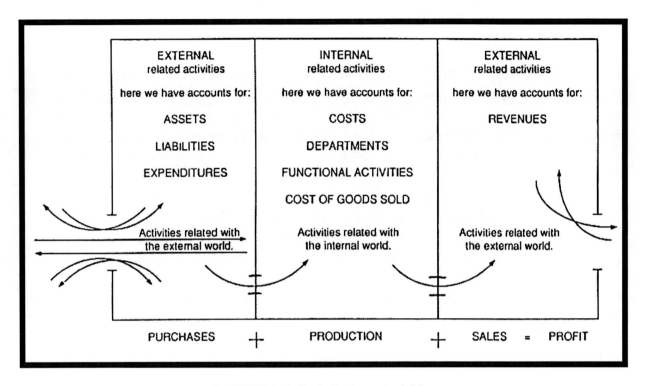

EXHIBIT 4--1: Basic Business Activities

Emanuel Schwarz

Here, also, the company interacts with the external world.

Exhibit 4--1 is simple, yet it reflects important business and accounting fundamentals: the operating results (profit or loss) are the consequence of the following activities:

PURCHASE + PRODUCTION + MARKETING = OPERATING RESULTS

To indicate more accurately basic business activities, it is important not to mix accounting situations or problems emanating from one activity with those of another. If a set of problems develops from the purchasing activity, that problem should not be transferred to the production activity; similarly, production activity problems should not be mixed with marketing activity problems.

> A vital functional concept should be evident:
> **Internal transactions of the company should be**
> **separated from external transactions of the company.**
> These two different activities must not be mixed.

In recognition of these two different activities, two separate control structures are essential to show two different accounting needs. When the external accounting transactions are separated from the internal accounting transactions, the company's management will understand better the cost accounting structure and see clearly the relationship to the basic needs for cost accounting and control.

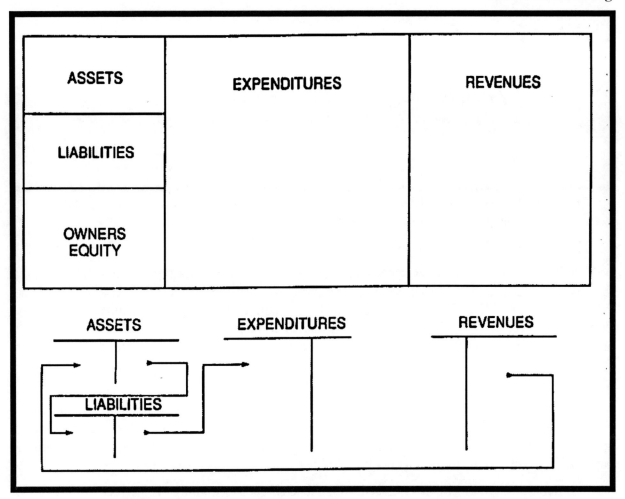

EXHIBIT 5--1: Basic Classification of Accounts for External Accounting.

CHAPTER 5

ACCOUNTING STRUCTURE

An accounting structure that decidedly separates external from internal accounting transactions is central to the Integrated Accounting System.

This is shown in Exhibits 5-1 and 5-2.

Exhibit 5--1 shows the three major classifications of accounts in a typical general accounting system and indicates the external accounting transactions. To the left, are the classes of accounts that represent the Balance Sheet accounts, that is, accounts for Assets, Liabilities, and Owners Equity. In the center of Exhibit 5--1, are the accounts corresponding to Expenditures. To the right are accounts related to Revenues. By matching amounts recorded under Expenditures for any specific period with those of the same period for Revenues, some measure of profit or loss can be identified.

All accounting transactions are identified and recorded within these classes of accounts. For example, to record an invoice (accrued), credit one liability account and debit one expenditure account. To record sales (accrued) requires a credit to Revenues and a debit to Assets. To record the payment of a debt, credit Assets and debit Liabilities.

The debit and credit circuit is closed with the General Accounting (Ext. Accounting) model shown in Exhibit 5--1.

When it is necessary to know the cost to produce a product, to sell it, to distribute it, and so on, one must, of course, consider the cost accounting approach. To determine the production cost, some new accounts must be devised in addition to those shown in Exhibit 5--1. These new accounts will function solely for Internal Accounting transactions, or Managerial Cost Accounting.

Exhibit 5--2 (see next page) is another illustration, and it describes the general nature of the Managerial Cost Accounting structure which the Integrated Accounting System will provide.

During a given period, an accountant must be able to identify how much the paid and/or accrued expenditures correspond to the production activity during this period. The portion of the expenditures which must be charged to the production activity, called COST ELEMENTS, is vital for true cost responsibility and is the core for the following basic and important concept:

COST ELEMENT = EXPIRED PORTION OF EXPENDITURE.

This means that the Internal Accounting model, as shown in Exhibit 5--2, must begin with Cost accounts (left side of Exhibit 5--2). Once the total cost has been identified for this accounting period, the following question must be answered:

How do these costs relate to the final functional activities of the company?

This restriction against transaction flow between internal and external accounting modules is not applicable to month-end i.e., end of the period activities.

Month end transactions have special rules that are described in another section of this book.

Exhibit 5--3 represents a graphic view of a General Accounting (External Accounting) system in a pictorial relationship to the Internal Accounting System.

This exhibit clearly shows the incorporation of the four classes of accounts representing the Internal Accounting system in their appropriate relationship between Expenditure and Revenues.

Turn to next page for Exhibit 5--3.

In the Integrated Accounting system, external and internal accounting models are realistically and judiciously fused into a single integrated structure.

This structural reality reflects a basic and significant difference between a traditional accounting system approach and the new Integrated Accounting System approach.

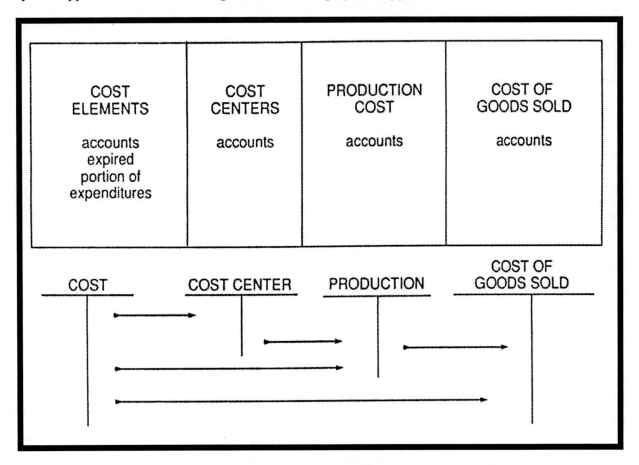

EXHIBIT 5--2: Basic Classification of Accounts for Internal Accounting.

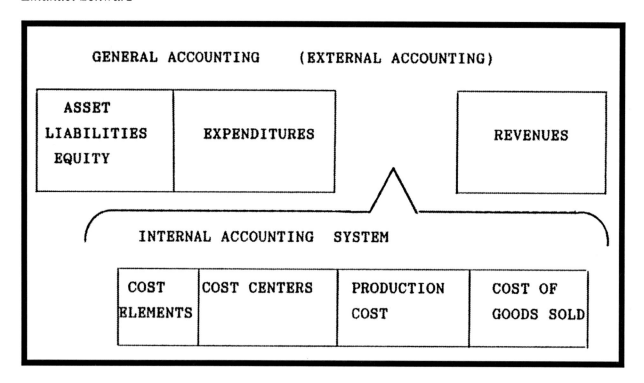

EXHIBIT 5--3: System Integration Process

The term "functional activities" includes not only the production activity, but also the support activities of maintenance, repair, and internal construction. Our question is quite relevant to the relationship of the cost to the functional activities. The "cost relationship to functional activities" can be analyzed further by answering two other questions:

Which costs have a **DIRECT** relationship to production?
Which costs have an **INDIRECT** relationship to production?
At this point, it is helpful to define the terms, direct and indirect:
DIRECT COSTS are those that change in proportion to changes in activity level.
INDIRECT COSTS are those that do not change in   proportion to changes in activity level.

It is not adequate to use these terms with two different interpretations. For example, we should not use the term direct cost for both those amounts that should be allocated to departments (Overhead) and those to be allocated directly to the production. This is giving the same term two different meanings. Every time we say that this cost is a direct one, we must clarify that we refer to a cost that must be charged to some department, or we have to indicate that this cost must be allocated to a production account.

Therefore, we recommend that these terms "Direct and Indirect" should always refer to the relationship of cost to of cost to the functional activity. The principal functional activity in an industry, is generally the production. We now have appropriate terminology: the Direct Cost will always be directly related to the functional activity, and the Indirect Cost will refer to cost that is to be charged to various departments.

These established terms will also help us to identify the next two terms:

Variable and the Fixed Cost.

The Direct Cost will always be a Variable Cost, because the Variable Cost should vary in proportion to changes in the functional activity level. And the activity level in this context means the same as the functional activity. Consequently, the Indirect Cost should always be identified as a fixed cost, which we have to allocate to various specific departments.

To teach that we allocate to the departments both fixed and variable cost creates confusion. If we analyze any cost and identify it as variable and charge it to some department, we clearly cannot state that these costs vary proportional to the changes in the functional activity.

This concept is demonstrated in Exhibit 5-2, which shows the Cost Center accounts immediately following the Cost Element accounts, and immediately preceding the Production Cost accounts.

The fourth and final segment of the Internal Accounting model is shown in Exhibit 5-2 at the far right side of the model as "Cost of Goods Sold." These four segments shown in the Internal Accounting model are the basic classifications necessary to fulfill the needs of control and costing in the Integrated Accounting (or Managerial cost) system. The result of the logic of this Internal Accounting System model is that, in a manner similar to External Accounting, a closed system of credits and debits is established.

What is the significance of this logical sequence?

Briefly, any cost amount that is credited to one of the segments of the Internal Accounting System model, such as Cost Element accounts, must consequently be debited in one of the other segments of the Internal Accounting System model. Similarly, any amount credited in an external account must have offsetting debits within the external account.

CHAPTER 6

STRUCTURAL CONSIDERATIONS

The establishment of a specific class of accounts - the Expenditures that identifies paid and/or accrued expenditures on a periodic basis (or the accounting period) enhances the External Accounting segment. The Expenditure budget will utilize this class of accounts, and the development of the company's cash outflow will consequently use both actual and budgeted amounts.

The following basic accounting methodology is used as a model for discussion:

+All invoices received should be credited to Accounts Payable, and the debit should be applied against the appropriate Expenditure account. It should be noted that the treatment of certain transactions under the traditional system would require, in some cases, the debiting of amounts against asset accounts. This is exactly what the Integrated Accounting System endeavors the Integrated Accounting

System endeavors to avoid by creating a specific class of accounts related to the expenditures.

+All checks processed for payment should be credited to the applicable bank account and debited to the corresponding Accounts Payable.

During the basic review of each invoice received for processing in the Accounts Payable unit, it is important to identify how much of the total amount of the expenditure is related to the Internal Accounting transactions. In other words, segregate the Expired and Un-expired portions of each expenditure. The employee who is responsible for coding invoices, in accordance with a given accounting methodology, will make basic decisions to determine the amounts of expenditures that are relative to this period's costs whether they are part of the cost, all of it, or none of it. The amounts to be charged to Internal Accounting must be indicated on the appropriate documents by the responsible employee.

Amounts that have been identified as Internal Accounting transactions will be credited to Cost Element accounts. These accounts belong to the very first classification of accounts established in the Internal Accounting System structure. Corresponding debits for each individual transaction relating to the credits mentioned above may be allocated to one or a number of Cost Center accounts (departments). The purpose is, of course, to follow the principle that if amounts are credited to Cost Elements, then it must be determined which account will receive the corresponding debits.

Here we have brought to the reader's attention the basic procedure that a modern accounting system will have to develop. This will be a system which would have both General and Internal Accounting. In previous chapters, we have established a clear picture that our cost-flow and, consequently, also our Chart of Accounts, must show a precise separation between accounting transactions related to External Accounting and those relating to Internal Accounting.

Here again let us analyze a graphic presentation as shown in one of the current Cost Accounting books. This time we will use the diagram of a Job Cost System presented in Professor Horngren/Foster's book, <u>Cost Accounting,</u> 1987, Prentice Hall.

We can see this presentation as Exhibit 6-1 on the next page. Here we can observe clearly that this cost accounting book develops a Job Cost System diagram within the General Accounting framework. It is obvious that a Job Cost system refers to accounting transactions that belong to the Internal Accounting exclusively. Obviously, we should not have this type of graphic presentation within the General Accounting. And the truth is, we do not have any other alternative but to use this present General Accounting structure.

Exhibit 6-1 illustrates clearly the need to separate External Accounting from Internal Accounting. A basic analysis shows that we credit Stores Control account which belongs to the Assets and transfer the corresponding amounts to the Work-in-Process Control and to the Factory Department Overhead Control accounts. Here again we may observe that the term "Work-in-Process Control account" is very inadequate because we actually do not like to control the amount of Work-in-Process at the moment when we finish the accounting period. Rather, we prefer to know the production cost for this job order.

This account shows us that this job order costs us a total of $ 48,999 in raw material, $ 39,000 in direct labor and $ 26,460 in absorbed overhead costs. These amounts were charged to this job order during this month. Of these values, a total amount of $ 108,800 was transferred to the Finished Goods Control account. As a consequence, the amount of work in process at the end of the month was only $ 4,660.

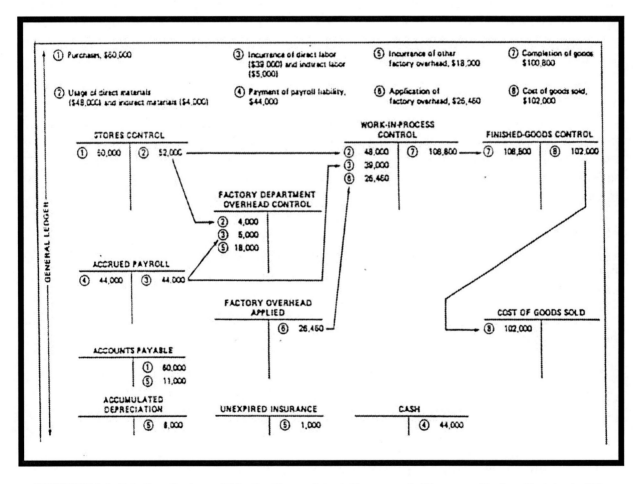

EXHIBIT 6-1: Job Cost System within the General Acct. Framework (Horngren/Foster: Cost Acctg.87)

We can see here very clearly that the Work-in-Process account should be identified by another name. The account represents the production cost of this job order. The inadequate term that we have today has its obvious origin in the fact that this account is located within the Assets of a company. Many professors refer to this account as an inventory of Work-in-Process. And having this account within the Assets, it could not be called Production Cost.

The actual production cost amount should be recorded outside the Balance accounts. This Production Cost account needs to be placed in a special class of accounts within the Internal Accounting. Here we would like to mention that within the inventory accounts, there must naturally be an account that will show the amount that was in process when we finished the accounting period. This account would be called "Work-in-Process," because it would indicate the difference between the amounts debited and credited to the Production Cost account in our Internal Accounting. In Chapter 15 we will discuss in detail the problems related to work in process.

The same problematic situation of having to credit External Accounting and transfer debit to Internal Accounting, is also created with the Accrued Payroll account as is recorded in Exhibit 6-1. Here again we credit a balance account and transfer the amount to an internal account: to the Factory Department Overhead control and to the Work-in-Process control. Here we have a greater problem: in our liability account of Accrued Payroll, we may have to credit a different amount than what would correspond to the Internal Accounting for this specific month. In this situation, we can see more clearly how important it is to separate the external transactions from the internal transactions.

Professor Horngren's presentation (Exhibit 6-1) is very interesting. In this exhibit, he indicates that we should have two accounts related to the Factory Department Overhead, one which will receive the actual allocated values to the department and another one that will be credited with the amount which we will have to apply to the job order (Work-in-Process). This is a perfect buildup of pure accounts. For example one account will show the actual allocated amounts, and the other will have the calculated amount. This idea is followed by the Integrated Accounting System, which we are presenting to the reader.

THE NEW DEVELOPMENT.

Now let us see how we could change today's structure so we can avoid the problems described above as well as many other problems. Let us see the cost-flow development that will give us a solution to the needs of both External and Internal Accounting.

We have established that we must basically separate the External Accounting transactions from the Internal ones. Let us analyze how the cost-flow should function within the General Accounting:

1. The cost-flow must refer to Assets, Liability, Expenditure, and Revenue accounts.

2. Among these specific accounts, the accounting flow moves clearly and logically.

Graphically we may show it as presented in Exhibit 6-2.

From Accounts Payable, the flow moves toward Expenditure Accounts. It is important to observe that within this class of accounts (Expenditures), we open all the types of expenditures that a firm may possibly have. All expenditures are those which we would identify within the Chart of

Accounts. That means that expenditures such as those related to the purchase of raw materials, parts, machinery, etc. also would be listed within this class of accounts. This procedure would make it possible to have all outflow amounts within one classification.

If we purchase raw material for our company, this amount must be charged to the Store's Purchase Account, just as we would charge the purchase of a pen set for a manager to the corresponding expenditure account. This first recording from A/P to Expenditure must be handled in both cases in the same way. From the point of view of outflow, there is no difference if we purchase raw material or a pen set. The total amount that we spend for this pen set will be taken as expired expenditure for cost purposes. If the total amount that we spent for the raw material was used up in the production, we will take this amount as expired expenditure for cost purposes.

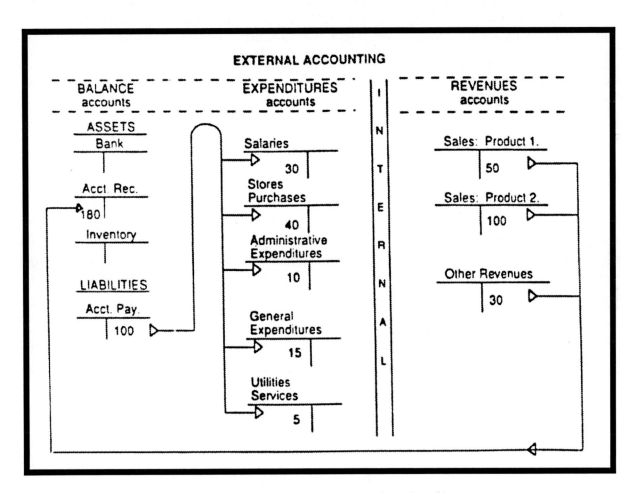

EXHIBIT 6-2: External Accounting Cost-flow Chart

But if some amount of raw material still is available at the end of the month, we naturally will record this amount as part of our Assets.

We have to use the same procedures for the purchase of machines, equipment or other so-called Fixed Assets.

Now we have created a new class of accounts that will give us the total picture of the accrued Expenditure of the month. Another accounting step will tell us if these Expenditures have been paid or not.

In Chapter 19, we will discuss the question of the month-end closing transactions.

In Exhibit 6-2, we can also see that the Revenue accounts transfer their amounts to an Asset Account. These two classes of accounts Expenditures and Revenues represent exactly what we read in the "Management Accounting Terminology" presented by the National Association of Accountants, Statement Number 2, June 1, 1983. We quote the description given for Accrual Basis:

A process whereby revenue is recognized as services are performed and expenses are recognized as efforts are expended or services used, regardless of when cash is received or disbursed.

This would be the whole transaction flow for External Accounting referring to the daily recording entries.

Our next question then would be:

How should we develop the Internal Accounting structure?

As we studied in previous chapters, we will have to start with the amounts that correspond to the expired portions of the Expenditures. Here we refer to the whole philosophy of matching the costs with the production of the month. We should not charge to Internal Accounting amounts that do not correspond as an internal cost of the company or that do not match with this month's functional activities. Here the matching does NOT refer to the revenues of the month.

The easiest way to structure the first class of accounts in the Internal Accounting would be to mirror copy the accounts we have developed in the External class. Let's analyze the following exhibit:

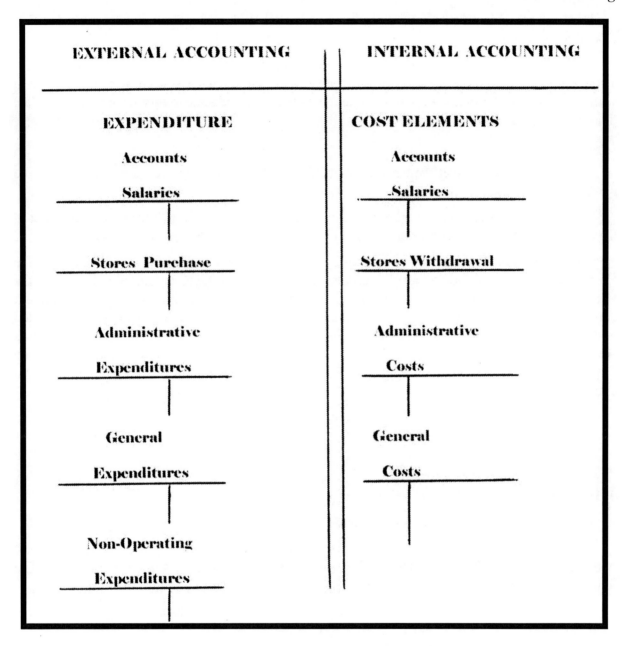

EXHIBIT 6-3: External and Internal Links.

Here we have identified a few expenditure accounts. Within this class we also record a Non Operating expenditure.

For each of the other expenditure accounts, we have to open a COST ELEMENT Account. Therefore, only the Non Operating expenditure account will not have a corresponding account within the Internal Accounting because the amounts which we allocate to this account do not relate to Internal Accounting.

We may also observe that some names in the COST ELEMENTS class do not correspond to the names in the Expenditure class.

It is a logical consequence: In the Expenditure class we use the term of "Stores Purchase," but in the Cost Element class, the corresponding account will show us the "Stores Withdrawal."

The same logic will be applied to the Expenditure class account of Fixed Assets Purchase. In the Cost Element class we would call this corresponding account, Depreciation. We allocate to the Expenditure Accounts the accrued amount. Then we have to analyze how much of this amount corresponds as the expired portion to the Internal Accounting. This expired portion will be credited to the COST ELEMENT class. Here we see the same philosophy of having two "pure" accounts as we observed in Exhibit 6-1, the two Factory Department accounts. We should not use the same Expenditure account for the expired portion. Neither should we mix in one account accrued and expired values.

Our next question will be: Where do we charge these amounts that we credited to our COST accounts?

THE INTERNAL ACCOUNTING STRUCTURE.

Let us now analyze, how we should structure the internal accounting.

At this present moment we know that the COST ELEMENT accounts must be the very first within the Internal Accounting. This is the outcome of what we have seen in Exhibit 6-3. The logical conclusion is: Internal Accounting must start with the expired portion of the Expenditure.

In the COST ELEMENTS class, we now have recorded all the costs which match with this accounting period and correspond to its production volume.

Where do these costs belong within our internal activities? To establish a clear analysis, we need to produce a logical base structure. Let us refer to the Final Cost Objective.

As a basic rule, we may say that the Final Cost Objective in any industry is the product. We refer clearly to the internal activity of this industry. Based upon this, we must analyze our Cost Elements in reference to the Final Cost Objective. The relationship will be as follows:

1. If the cost has a direct link with the product, that cost must be allocated directly to the product's account. This cost is subsequently identified as a **Direct Cost.**

2. If the cost has NO direct link with the product, that cost should NOT be allocated directly to the product. This cost is an **Indirect Cost.** These costs will be allocated to different departments.

All Cost Elements within Internal Accounting must be <u>allocated.</u> The first step in this procedure is to allocate all Indirect Costs to the various departments.

The next step will be to allocate the Direct Costs to the Production Cost accounts, or to the different Functional Activities.

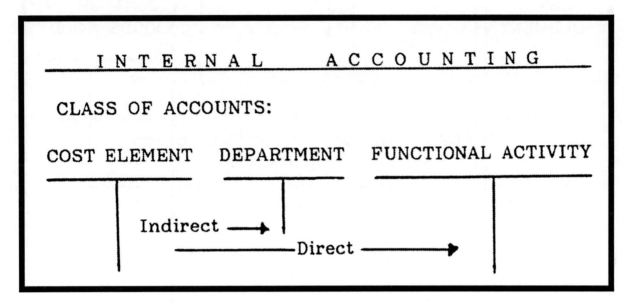

EXHIBIT 6-4: Allocation of Direct and Indirect Costs.

In this graphic example we have the two most important basic allocation steps within our Internal Accounting. There is a third step: The allocation of Cost of Goods Sold. From the Class of Cost Elements, we transfer the amount of the goods sold to a specific class within the Internal Accounting which we call, Cost of Goods Sold.

Thus, there are three basic ALLOCATION steps:

1. Indirect Cost allocated to the departments.

2. Direct Cost allocated to the Functional Activities.

3. Allocation of the Cost of Goods Sold.

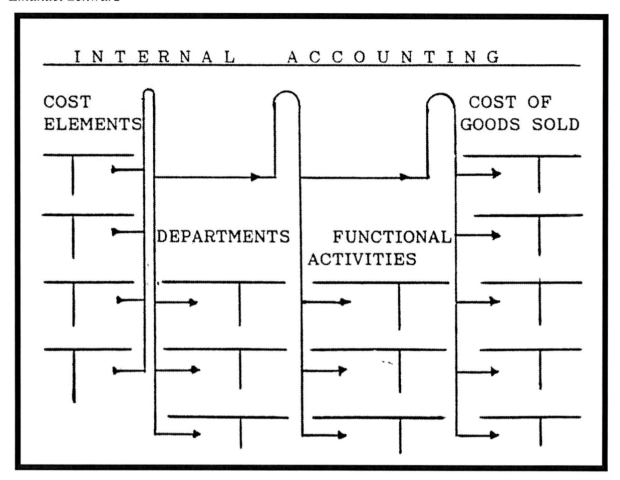

EXHIBIT 6-5: Cost Allocation

With the explanations of the Allocation steps, we have established the cost-flow structure of Internal Accounting. It is the same structure we discussed in the previous chapter and the corresponding Exhibits No 5-1, 5-2, and 5-3.

In the following chapters, we will clarify the problems of reallocation and of cost absorption.

CHAPTER 7

DEPARTMENTAL OPERATING COST

In the beginning of this book, we discussed how the Owners Equity account was subdivided into Expense and Revenue accounts. For many years the accounting was recorded in large-columned books, giving necessary information about the different expenses that the company had incurred.

Subsequently, management observed the need for having control over the expenses incurred by each department. And a RESPONSIBILITY accounting system was created. Within the Financial cost flow structure the question remained, where should these new accounts be located. It was not an easy problem to solve because within the Financial cost frame, no space was left for such new accounts as we have had to deal with here.

Let us look at the following graphic diagram which shows the general rules of accounting transactions. This diagram is taken from the book Principles of Financial and Managerial Accounting, by Professors Carl S. Warren and Philip E. Fess (Southwestern Publishing Co. 1986).

As shown in Exhibit 7-1, it is an excellent presentation of the structure of General Accounting. The most logical approach would have been to open these new responsibility accounts after Expense accounts.

Emanuel Schwarz

The business transactions of Ingram Corporation are summarized by the accounting equation and accounts as follows. The transactions are identified by letter, and the balance of each account at the end of the month is shown.

Assets	=	Liabilities	+	Owner's Equity	SUMMARY OF TRANSACTIONS

Cash

(a) 60,000	(c) 8,000
(d) 62,000	(e) 43,500
70,500 122,000	51,500

Supplies

(b) 12,000	(f) 7,500
4,500	

Accounts Payable

(c) 8,000	(b) 12,000
	4,000

Capital Stock

	(a) 60,000

Fees Earned

	(d) 62,000

Wages Expense

(e) 25,000	

Rent Expense

(e) 10,000	

Supplies Expense

(f) 7,500	

Utilities Expense

(e) 6,000	

Miscellaneous Expense

(e) 2,500	

EXHIBIT 7-1: The Accounting Equation

And this solution would have carried us directly into the "world" of Internal accounting. But at that time in the development of the accounting profession, this step was unacceptable. Only Professor Maurice L. Hirsh, Jr. and Joseph G. Louderback III show in their book <u>COST ACCOUNTING,</u> second edition, Kent Publishing Co, 1986, the same basic idea of having the Overhead cost after the Expense accounts. Exhibit 7-2 shows this presentation. But this graphic was never developed in a complete picture of the cost-flow.

The solution that was finally adopted was simple and at the same time very drastic: Just forget the Expense accounts and in their place, put in the new accounts for the needs of the Responsibility Accounting system. "What name should we give to these accounts?" was the logical question.

And someone said:" Let's call them OVERHEAD."

Let us now see which are Overhead Costs in accordance with Statement Number 2 of June 1, 1983 and published as the Management Accounting Terminology by the NAA:

"Those costs which cannot, as a practical matter, be assigned to a firm's objectives in a direct fashion; overhead costs are, however, related to the accomplishment of those objectives."

These costs are, in an indirect fashion, related to the final cost objective of our functional activities. Therefore, we may call these amounts INDIRECT costs.

Simply stated, these costs will not change proportionally to the changes of the functional activity to which they refer. They are, in other words, basically fixed costs.

But unpleasant realities remain:

1. We have to teach accounting students that we open Expense Accounts for explicit information within the Owner's Equity Accounts.

2. We also have to teach that these Expense Accounts disappear as soon as we develop a more advanced accounting system; that these Expense Accounts are now replaced with Overhead Accounts; and that these Overhead accounts do not count in the Balance sheet or in the Income Statement.

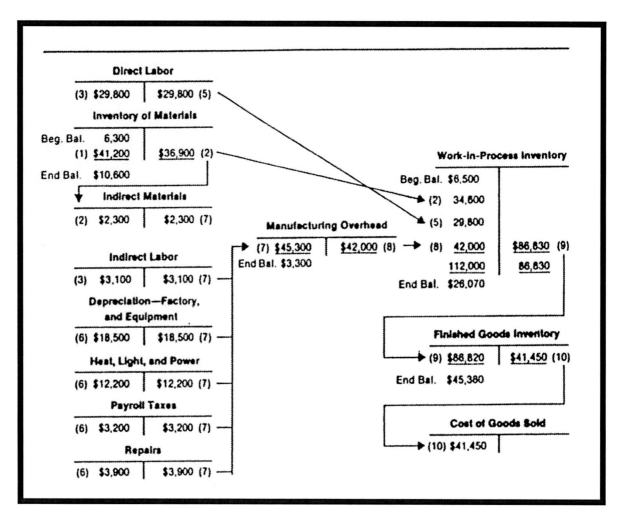

EXHIBIT 7-2: Transfer of Expenses to Overhead

To understand this better, let us look again closely at Exhibit 6-1, where we can see that we transfer from an Asset or Liability account, amounts directly to the Factory Department Overhead Control account. In this graphic presentation we have lost the Expense Accounts which we prepared in our Principles of Accounting study.

The confusion of having Expense Accounts and not showing them, and having Overhead Accounts and not using them, in the minds of many managers and many accountants, is our present unfortunate situation. We have no clear graphic structure to explain the actual cost-flow in our Internal Accounting System.

DEPARTMENT CONFIGURATION

Referring back to what we have just discussed, we can see clearly that we need a special cost-flow structure for Internal Accounting. We start this Internal Accounting with the class of accounts that we identify as COST ELEMENTS, i.e., the expired portion of the Expenditures. If these Costs are indirectly related to the functional activities of our company, we allocate them to the different departments within our company. The Responsibility Accounting System of today refers only to the production and service departments of our company. We totally neglect the responsibility control of the administrative and sales departments. This present procedure requires change in order to include all departments of our company in this Responsibility Accounting System.

The configuration of the class of accounts that will represent the departments of our company must have at least the following basic groups of accounts:

1. Administrative and Sales Departments

2. Direct Production Departments

3. Indirect Production Departments, and

4. Service Departments.

Nearly all companies will need to have these four groups of departments. Very seldom will a company have no Service Department or no Indirect Production Department.

The Administrative Department group includes all general administrative units. It should not include administrative production departments, such as supervisory units, but may include the Production Manager's Department. The Sales would include such units as Raw material Inventory, Finished Goods Inventory, Purchasing Department and Delivery units.

Here is the challenge: To balance in an adequate way all departments of the company. After the very first structure of this class of accounts, we have to test this configuration after the first year and introduce the necessary changes. It becomes a real live, dynamic structure.

The second group of accounts includes the most important departments of our company: the Direct Production departments. That means that we have to identify within this group all those departments which are working directly with the production. Occasionally it will be necessary to open specific Main accounts which will represent several departments related to the same activity. Heading these production units, would be the engineering and supervisory departments.

The third group of accounts includes those departments that are working indirectly with the production such as maintenance and repair. Quality control, configuration control, and research and development departments would also be included in Indirect Production Department. Here again, is the question of analyzing the correct structure and relationship of the department.

Finally, we have the group of Service Department. This group includes such units as janitorial, medical, security, etc. This department will have to be treated in a special way because we will have to reallocate the amounts which we have charged to it, to those departments to which it have given its service. We will talk about this point later in this chapter.

ALLOCATION PROCEDURE

The procedure for allocation of the indirect cost to the department is basically very simple. When the accountant who prepared the accounting system and its procedures, some basic rules to guide the accounting of this allocation had to be established.. The rules presented here give instructions regarding costs that can be clearly identified as the operating costs of a specific department and should be allocated to this department. Examples of such identifiable costs are: salaries for supervisors and other personnel of the departments, wages that correspond to personnel who are not directly engaged in the production work, rent that can be prorated to the department, office supplies for that department, depreciation that corresponds to the machines within the department, other fixed assets, etc.

And we will also find some indirect costs that will not be so easy to allocate to a specific department. A telephone bill that does not refer to a specific number located in a department, for example. The company may have a switchboard and consequently it would be difficult to relate the bill to any specific department. In this case, we may establish two different approaches:

1. Allocate the total phone bill to only one department, such as the General Manager.

2. Allocate some pre-established percentage of the bill to several specific departments.

This percentage allocation method will have to be revised every year and, as necessary, changed to more correct conditions.

It is important to point out that we should generally not prepare some type of intricate allocation system. It is probably not worth the effort. The whole purpose of this indirect cost allocation is to keep it simple but effective and to give management an accurate and reliable operating cost picture of the different departments.

Most of these indirect costs belong to the group of fixed costs. But we will also have some costs that can logically be allocated to the departments (especially direct production) and which could be identified as variable costs. Typically these include costs such as screws, bolts, etc., which vary proportionally with the level of production.

Let us look at the following example:

A department is assembling refrigerators. For each unit they need 16 screws and 4 bolts of specific dimensions. The assemblers will not receive the exact quantity of these screws and bolts needed for one day's production. These parts will be received in large quantities, perhaps a case. The cost of a case of the screws will have to be charged to the operating cost of the department, and later this cost will be absorbed partially or in total by the different job orders that were produced during this day. We will discuss the absorption concept and procedure in the next chapter.

Naturally, actual costs allocated to specific departments will be compared with the departments budgeted amounts. We are aware that the budget is not accounting, but management data that is prepared outside of the accounting system. The Internal Accounting structure, however, is the first system that will have a class of accounts that may be compared directly to the budgeted departmental operating costs.

The first two classes of accounts COST ELEMENTS and DEPARTMENTS that we have discussed here are the initial building blocks of Internal Accounting.

WE ARE NOW GAINING RELEVANCE IN OUR ACCOUNTING STRUCTURE.

DIRECT LABOR WAGE.

Direct labor wages are normally taken as a variable cost and consequently charged directly to the Production Cost Account (what currently is Work in Process). It is said that the direct labor wages will change proportionally to the changes of the production level. But if we correctly analyze the structure of these wages, we will most likely come to the conclusion that this payment is only related to the time period of one hour; i.e., one hour at work, one hour pay received. This payment is earned, not because the worker dedicated time to produce something, but simply by being present at the job place or work station. Very few industries pay their workers only per unit of production (often called piece work).

This means actually that direct labor wage is a fixed cost just as the salary is a fixed cost. There is only a difference in time span: for example, salary per month and wage per hour.

Obviously, we should allocate the direct labor wage to the corresponding Direct Production department. Only Direct Production departments will have direct labor wages. The amount to be allocated to such departments will be related to the total earned direct labor hours. This will be the actual cost of direct labor recognized to this Direct Production department. This amount may also be compared with the budgeted costs for management purpose.

The next step is to identify how much of this actual direct labor wage is to be <u>absorbed</u> by the different Job orders. The amount will vary proportionately with the activity level of the production. We may conclude, that the <u>absorbed</u> direct labor wage is the variable cost of the production.

This brings us to the next step of development: a new class of accounts related to the Functional Activities of the company. But before we enter into this discussion, let us finish this chapter with following observations.

REALLOCATION OF COSTS

We <u>allocate</u> the appropriate operating costs to Service Departments. As mentioned before, we have departments such as maintenance. Let us look at the following example:

The budgeted operating cost of the maintenance department was established at an amount of $ 10,000 per month. Included in the budgeted costs were salaries, wages, rent, depreciation, insurance, office supplies, etc. The actual departmental operating costs were allocated to this department, but they will NOT be absorbed by the production because no relationship exists between the departmental costs and the production activity, yet this service department <u>did</u> have

Emanuel Schwarz

these operating costs because it served other departments with its activity. Consequently, the most logical procedure will be to REALLOCATE these operating costs to departments served.

We will use the term REALLOCATION so that we have a clear distinction between the first step of allocation and this new step of reallocation. When we prepare the budget of the Service Department, we have to identify the most correct

reallocation base. It will not always be easy to find this reallocation base, but here again we do not have to develop a sophisticated system, just a clear and reasonable identification of how these service costs could be reallocated. We will need to, therefore, establish monthly amounts that will be reallocated to the different departments served. Every year these reallocated amounts will be verified with the actual conditions, and as appropriate, they will be changed.

These reallocated amounts will be credited to a specific account that will have only the reallocated values. The actual departmental operating costs will be debited to the corresponding departmental account. The variance between the actual and the budgeted reallocated amount will guide supervisors and managers in their efforts to control departmental operating costs.

Exhibit 7-3 shows a graphic presentation of the reallocation concept just discussed.

As can be seen in Exhibit 7-3, we have opened two classes of accounts: one class to charge the operating costs TO the departments, and one used to transfer these operating costs FROM the departments.

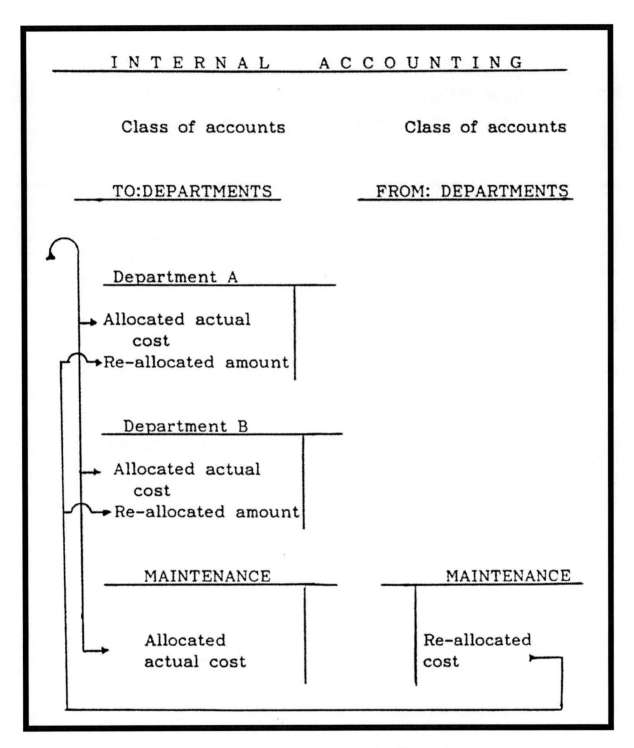

EXHIBIT 7-3: Service Departments Cost Transactions.

CHAPTER 8

ABSORPTION OF DEPARTMENTAL OPERATING COSTS

Exhibit 7-3 shows a new detail of the Internal Accounting structure. Besides having the Class of Accounts that will refer to specific Departments, we clearly need another Class of Accounts that will be used only for the absorbed (applied) amounts. Recall that Professor Horngren developed this idea in his graph shown in Exhibit 6-1, which we follow in principle. Hence, we will place two differently structured amounts in two accounts:

One account: for the **actual departmental operating costs**

One account: for the **absorbed operating costs.**

Consequently, we call the first Class of Accounts "TO: DEPARTMENTS" amounts that we will charge <u>to</u> the different departments.

The next Class of Accounts are called "FROM: DEPARTMENTS" absorbed amounts that will be taken <u>from</u> these departments to the receiving ones.

Studying Exhibit 8-1 provides a clear picture of the Internal Accounting structure.

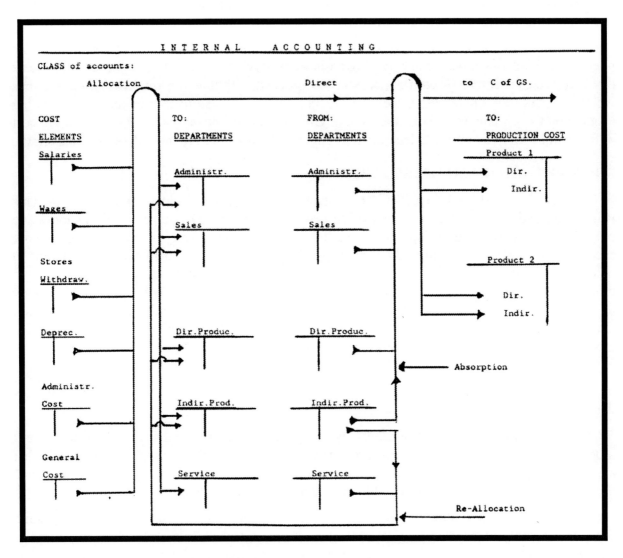

EXHIBIT 8-1: Internal Cost Structure.

To the left of Exhibit 8-1, we have the first Class of Accounts, identified as COST ELEMENTS. From here we allocate the direct and indirect costs to the Production Cost account and to specific departments of the company.

Cost allocation is the first step necessary to start our internal accounting transactions. The next step will be to reallocate the operating costs from Service Departments to those departments that received the service. Then it is necessary to proceed with the Absorption Cost transactions which will take the operating cost of the Direct Production departments to the corresponding Production Cost accounts. Finally, the Cost of Goods Sold will have to absorb the operating cost of the Administrative and Sales departments. This will be presented in more detail in Chapter 10.

SOME DETAILS OF COST ABSORPTION

In this Exhibit 8-1 we have actually designated only one Direct Production department. This is a simplification of the real world situation because a business or company will seldom have only one Direct Production department. In any case, the point here is, we have to prepare according to our cost accounting books one predetermined absorption rate. It is important to note, however, that we need to indicate that we may have to use several such absorption rates to transfer the departmental operating costs to the different products. One such absorption rate may use the direct labor hours as a distribution base; another may use the machine hours; and another, may use some other base. Let us remember that for each Direct Production department, we have to study these individual rates to determine the appropriate rate.

When our accounting system was handled manually, we were not physically able to employ more than one absorption rate. Now with the use of computers, we may manipulate several rates that incorporate many necessary details.

Within the Production Cost accounts, we may have accounts referring to each and every product (or product groups), and each product will have to identify the specific job orders that are assigned to it. In no way must we charge these departmental operating costs to only one product account. This will be discussed in more detail in the next chapter.

We have also some Indirect Production departments whose costs must be absorbed by some functional activity of our company. Within this group of departments are such cost centers as maintenance and repair. For these departments, we also have to establish some absorption rates which, occasionally, is difficult. The operating costs of the maintenance department must be charged to the different maintenance activities. In some companies, maintenance is highly important, in which case, we will have to prepare a preventive maintenance budget. Such maintenance budget work helps to establish the absorption rates for the department. Here again we must remember that it is not necessary to prepare a complicated absorption system. A simple structure will give adequate information. After a year or two of use, it may be appropriate and desirable to develop a more complex absorption system.

If there is a quality control department, we may have to realize a reallocation of these operating costs to those departments which receive quality control services. A research department requires that its costs be applied to the different projects on which it is working. These project accounts would have to be established within the Functional Activity Class of accounts. As we have observed, there will always be some variances between the actual departmental operating costs and the absorbed amounts. These points discussed in Chapter 19.

CHAPTER 9

FUNCTIONAL
ACTIVITY ACCOUNTS

In this chapter we will discuss the most important part of the Internal Accounting structure: Functional Activity accounts. Developing this class of accounts will give management essential information about the PRODUCTION COST.

In this class of accounts we will not only control production types of costs, but also the cost related to maintenance, repair, and internal production. By internal production we refer to that production which the firm develops for its own use such as tools, machines, construction of a building, etc.

The <u>entire</u> operation of our company will be described within the Functional Activities, and these different activities are the final cost objectives of our firm.

The Functional Activity accounts will give us the detailed information of how much Direct Cost we charged to a specific job order or process, how much of Indirect Cost was absorbed by this job order or process, and how much of the production was transferred to Inventory of Finished Goods.

It is important to be clear that the structure of the Functional Activity accounts is also divided into two Classes the same type of division used to develop the Departmental Operating Class of accounts: One Class refers to charged amounts and another Class refers to amounts transferred to some receiving accounts. In Exhibit 9-1 (on next page), both Classes of Accounts belong to Functional Activities. The first class, on the left, will have only those accounts that receive the corresponding amounts to be charged to the different activities. The next class will have only those accounts that are to be credited with the amounts that will be transferred to some receiving accounts, in this case inventory of goods.

The first group within these classes contains accounts that we will use to control the production cost. Within this group we have Main accounts and Sub-accounts which are to be used to control a specific product cost, identified by each Job order. For example, an account which corresponds to Production No.1 and Job order No. 22 will be charged with the amount of raw material used to fulfill this order. Similarly, the amount that corresponds to Direct Labor Wages and the absorbed (indirect) cost, will be charged to this specific account.

When we refer to a Job order system, the calendar month it takes to produce it is less important. What is referred to with a Job order is independent of the amount of days of a month spent in this Job order; we will accumulate, day after day, week after week, all costs that refer to this Job order.

The job may be worked during more than just a one month period. Details about how we transfer Job order costs from month to month, will be discussed in Chapter 15.

In the Class of Accounts to the right in Exhibit 9-1, the first Group is identified as FROM: PRODUCTION. It should have the same Main accounts and Sub accounts as the accounts in the TO: PRODUCTION. The accounts in these two Classes run parallel and should have the same name and the same code. The amount that we credit to this account will be the value of the products finished and transferred to the Inventory of Finished Goods. Obviously, the question will be how to establish this amount. And the most correct response is, we have to work with Standard Cost System.

```
INTERNAL          ACCOUNTING
```

CLASS of accounts:

Functional	Activity	Accounts

GROUP: TO: FROM:

PRODUCTION   PRODUCTION

Product # 1		Product # 1	
Job-Order # 22		Job-Order # 22	
Raw Mat.	x	Transfer	
Dir. Lab.	x	to	
Absorbed	x	Inventory	
total	x	total	y

GROUP: TO: FROM:

MAINTENANCE   MAINTENANCE

Building # 3		Building # 3	
Material	x	Transfer	
Labor	x	to	
Absorbed	x	corr.accts.	
total	x	total	y

GROUP: TO: FROM:

REPAIR   REPAIR

Machine # 4		Machine # 4	
Job-Order # 5		Job-Order # 5	
Material	x	Transfer	
Labor	x	to	
Absorbed	x	corr.accts.	
total	x	total	y

GROUP: TO: FROM:

INTERNAL PROD.   INTERNAL PROD.

Job-Order # 7		Job-Order # 7	
Material	x	Transfer	
Labor	x	to	
Absorbed	x	corr.acct.	
total	x	total	y

EXHIBIT 9-1: Functional Activity Class

51

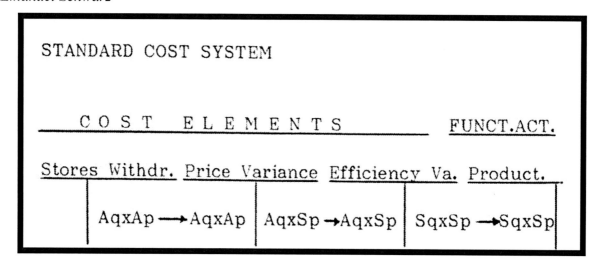

EXHIBIT 9-2: Standard Cost Accounts.

The Standard Cost Accounts is a very simple structure.

We recommend that the inventory of raw materials should be carried at actual price. Consequently, the withdrawal amounts will be made at actual quantity times actual price. This amount will be transferred to a special account within the Class of Cost Elements. We call this account: Price Variance. Price Variance is charged with the amount that we took out of the Store, and we will credit this account with the amount based upon the actual quantity times standard price. The difference will tell us the price variance and it will refer to the amount of raw material that we used in this Job order. The amount with which we credited this Price Variance account, we transfer to the next account that will show us the Efficiency Variance. We will credit this account with the amount that we receive by multiplying the Standard Quantity times Standard Price. The Standard quantity must refer to the Good Output of the production that actually occurred with this Job order. Finally, this last amount will be transferred to the Production Cost account in the Functional Activity Class.

The Standard Direct Labor cost would be developed in the same way, except we locate the Payment and Efficiency Variance accounts within the FROM: DEPARTMENTS Class of accounts. These details will be discussed in Chapter 14.

An important aspect of Internal Accounting is that companies should control production with Job orders. This is a very realistic and responsible way of controlling functional activities. At the same time, the Job order system is often a somewhat difficult procedure to work with. If management can see that some specific production should not be controlled by a Job order, it will have to accept some type of simplification, for example one Job order for several different production activities that are relatively small. In addition to work with Job orders, management should also introduce Standard Cost procedures. The Internal accounting structure we are presenting, however, does not depend upon having or not having Standard Costs.

MAINTENANCE AND REPAIR ACCOUNTS

The next group of accounts within the Functional Activity Class controls the maintenance and repair within the company. Sometimes we are required to prepare a preventive maintenance budget which makes it necessary to have special accounts that will correspond to these activities special building maintenance, vehicle maintenance, machine maintenance, for example. Here again, we should develop a system that will provide a practical service. And it is important, too, that our Internal Accounting system have the necessary capacity to give all these details if asked for.

Once we have charged to the maintenance account the corresponding material, labor, and absorbed amount, we have to question: "Where do we transfer these values?" If it is the maintenance of some specific building, we should reallocate the total amount to some management department that works within that building. We would have to credit the FROM: MAINTENANCE account and debit to the corresponding management department, TO: DEPARTMENTS class of accounts.

We recommend that same procedure for machine maintenance costs. A more specific step is required, however, if maintenance refers to some machine which produces specific Job orders. In this case, we have to find some certain baseline from which to charge maintenance to these Job orders. For this, machine hours could be used as a reallocation base.

Repair accounts can also be highly important. We need to know how to include repair costs as part of operating costs of our trucks, for example, and possibly for each important and expensive vehicle. We should also have the same point of view regarding machine repair. Expensive machines will need to have special repair accounts with detailed information about the spare parts cost, labor cost, and absorbed amounts. These repair costs will have to be reallocated to the Job orders that were produced by these machines, or to the Traffic, or Shipping and Receiving Department of the company.

Finally, we have a special Group of accounts that refer to the cost of internal production. Each internal production cost has a unique Job order. We include here such activities as producing our own machines, tools, or constructing our own building.

* * *

The Internal Accounting Structure has been used with great success in bridge and building construction projects. Each project had its Main account within specific groups. The different functional activities of each project were identified by Sub accounts and special Sub-sub accounts which provided more details within each activity.

EVALUATION.

We have discussed the most important Classes of accounts that must be built into the Internal Accounting structure of a company. This new picture of the internal cost-flow will give both students and managers a much better understanding of the necessity of developing internal transactions and how the different internal accounts will give us new and critical information. Those who understand accounting can readily observe the significant positive difference between what we have today as a cost-flow for internal use and what details are possible with the new Internal Accounting structure. These new classes of accounts give a much clearer picture of the Internal Accounting transactions.

Exhibit 9-3 on the following page shows the basic cost-flow structure for the new Internal Accounting System.

Emanuel Schwarz

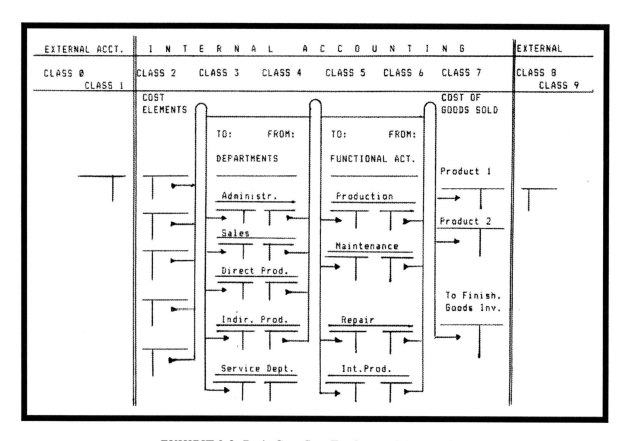

EXHIBIT 9-3: Basic Cost-flow For Internal Accounting.

CHAPTER 10

COST OF GOODS SOLD

This chapter explores a very interesting Class of Accounts: the COST OF GOODS SOLD. And we also have in this class other accounts that must be part of the Internal Accounting structure, and which are used as contra accounts within our cost-flow presentation.

Let us begin with the first Group of accounts within this class: the Cost of Goods Sold. The quantity and details of the accounts within this Group should be adjusted to the requirements of the sales activity. Here we may have Main accounts which have several Sub-accounts and these in turn have Sub-Sub-accounts. Generally, the Sub-Sub-account refers to an individual product or service; the Sub-account generally refers to a group of similar or related products; and the Main account is commonly organized by geographic areas or by groups of clients. It is important that we charge to these accounts, as appropriate, the cost of the goods sold.

HOW TO ESTABLISH THE COST OF GOODS SOLD.

The production cost that we established in the Functional Activity Class is transferred from the Production Cost account to the Finished Goods Inventory. This inventory account within Internal Accounting is a contra account to the Inventory of the Finished Goods in Assets. We mentioned before that daily transactions in External Accounting must be held separate from Internal Accounting. This means that if we credit some account in the Internal structure, we are not permitted to transfer this amount to debit in some External account. If we do so, we will not receive a correct trial balance in these two accounting systems.

The contra account of Finished Goods will transfer its balance to External Accounting only at the end of the month.

When we withdraw some finished goods from the inventory for the purpose of sales, the first recording from the source document (Inventory withdrawal) will have to be registered in Internal Accounting because it affects the company internally. The following Classes must be used:

FROM: COST ELEMENTS

TO: COST OF GOODS SOLD

The amount of goods withdrawn will be directly related to the quantity and the unit production cost. In no way should we accept that the cost of goods sold will refer to the difference between the debit amount in our Finished Goods Inventory and the ending inventory amount in the credit. This is only acceptable within Financial Accounting, for the Income Statement prepared for external readers. Managerial information must provide a more detailed report that is more representational and accurate.

For completeness, it is necessary to identify each unit sold and/or the group of the same units. With typical current computer software support, we should now always be able to work with perpetual inventory control.

Emanuel Schwarz

The value of each unit of the goods sold is a combination of the raw material, the direct labor, and the absorbed indirect costs. We may call this total value the manufacturing cost. But we have to accept, that besides this manufacturing cost, each company also has costs related to the sales and the administrative activities. We therefore recommend that these costs also be transferred to the Cost of Goods Sold. Here we have to establish a new absorption system: that would be the absorption base which we may use to charge the different sales and administrative costs to the accounts of Goods Sold.

The sales costs can be more easily identified in their relationship to the goods sold. Here we establish a specific absorption base. However, the relationship between administrative costs and the goods sold is more complicated. Unquestionably, a special study is needed to find the best absorption base. But again we must remember to develop and maintain a simple system in our Internal Accounting, a system that will give us as good and reliable information as is required, practical and acceptable.

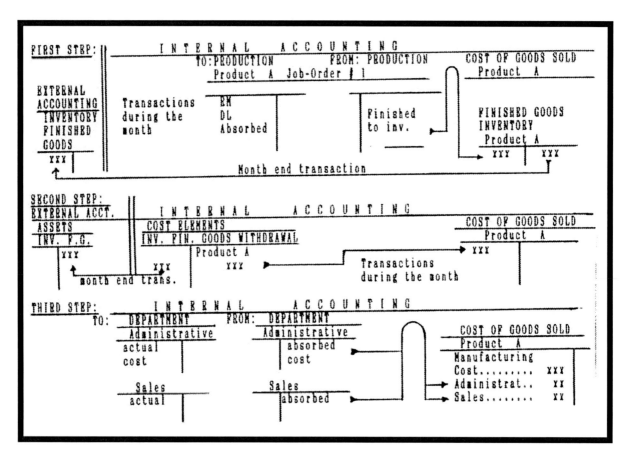

EXHIBIT 10-1: Finished Goods Transactions

Exhibit 10-1 shows a graphical presentation of the basic transactions that we discussed. We start with the first step: to take the production to the contra account of the Inventory of Finished Goods. The month-end transaction is also shown in this first step.

The second step shows the withdrawal of goods sold from the inventory account to the sales account. And the final step refers to the absorption transactions of administrative and sales costs. The important point here is, that we have to include in the Cost of Goods sold not only the manufacturing costs but also the Administrative and Sales costs.

Exhibit 10-1 shows three steps related to the establishment of Cost of Goods Sold.

FIRST STEP: From Production to the Inventory of Finished Goods, and month-end transactions to the Finished Goods account in Assets.

SECOND STEP: From Finished Goods Inventory account in the Internal Accounting to the Cost of Goods Sold.

THIRD STEP: Absorption of Administrative and Sales costs.

OTHER GROUPS WITHIN THIS CLASS OF ACCOUNTS

This last Class of accounts within the Internal Accounting contains not only the Group of accounts that represent the Cost of Goods Sold, but also the Internal Accounting needs for its cost-flow structure.

To maintain the double entry procedure within the Internal Accounting, we have to include in this last Class of accounts, the following Groups:

1.   INVENTORY Accounts

2.   REPAIR AND CONSTRUCTION Accounts

3.   TRANSFER Accounts.

INVENTORY ACCOUNTS.

Within the Inventory accounts Group we need to have accounts that will receive the cost of finished goods transferred from the production activity to the inventory. These Finished Goods Inventory accounts are contra accounts to the inventory account in the Assets. During the daily or weekly transactions, these accounts are used within this Class. At the end of each accounting period (month), it is necessary to transfer these amounts from Internal Accounting to External Accounting. This type of recording, from credit Internal to debit External, is for month-end transactions only.

Within the Inventory Accounts Group, are the Main accounts that refer to semi finished goods. Here we refer to a production cost, which coincides with the manufacturing of some component that we need in our industry. To these particular manufacturing costs, we should not add any administrative or sales activity costs.

REPAIR AND CONSTRUCTION ACCOUNTS.

The value of some major repairs will have to be recorded as part of Assets. We can control the repair cost within the Functional Activity Class of accounts. When we finish a specific major repair, we need to transfer the accumulated amount from the Functional Activity Class to an account within this Repair Group. At the end of each month this amount will have to be transferred to a machine inventory account in Assets.

Similar procedures must also be used for internal construction. The difference is that at the end of each month, the accumulated amount of the construction will always have to be transferred to a Construction in Process account in Assets. The construction account within the Functional Activity Class shows the monthly investment and the year to date amount.

TRANSFER ACCOUNTS

This last group of accounts will be used for transactions that have their origin within the Internal Accounting and which have to be transferred to the External Accounting. As an example we may look at the transfer of finished goods to some branch office. The first source document would be the inventory withdrawal of these products. We would credit the Cost Element Class account of Finished Goods Inventory and debit an account within this Group of Transfers. The month end transaction would take the amount from credit Transfers to debit Branch-Office Inventory account.

CHAPTER 11

TOTAL GRAPHIC PRESENTATION

A total graphic presentation of the Integrated Accounting System will illustrate just how complete a system it is.

This is shown in Exhibit 11-1, which details the whole structure.

In Exhibit 4-1, we identified the external transactions of the company on the left-hand side of that presentation. This pattern is followed at the top of the total graphic display of Exhibit 11-1.

The first lines of description in Exhibit 11-1 demonstrate that the first two Classes of accounts correspond to External Accounting. The next six Classes represent the total Internal Accounting the new internal cost-flow creation and to the right we again have two Classes that belong to the External Accounting system. Under this first description line are the names of the ten Classes into which the Integrated Accounting System is divided:

CLASS 0: represents all balance accounts: from Assets to Liabilities, ending with Capital / Equity accounts.

CLASS 1: identifies all **Expenditure** accounts. In this Class, expenditures are charged to specific accounts for all accrued invoices that are received.

CLASS 2: identifies all **Cost Element** accounts the beginning of the Internal Accounting. These amounts are the expired portions of the Expenditures.

CLASS 3 and 4: represent the **Departments** (Cost Centers).

Class 3 identifies only amounts charged TO Departments, Class 4 identifies only absorbed amounts FROM Departments. Only under special conditions and month-end transactions are there credits to the accounts of Class 3 and debits to Class 4.

CLASS 5 and 6: represent accounts related to the **Functional Activities** such as production, maintenance, repair, and construction. Class 5 accounts are used to identify only amounts charged TO Production. Class 6 accounts are used to identify only amounts transferred FROM Production.

CLASS 7: relates to **Cost of Goods Sold**. These accounts must be debited to the manufacturing costs. The credit of this amount corresponds to Stores Withdrawal in Cl.2. Class 7 also has accounts related to Finished Goods Inventory, accounts for Major Repairs, Construction, and Transfers.

CLASS 8: represents the collection of all **Revenues**, those related to normal activity, special sales and non-operating revenues.

CLASS 9: represents only the **Closing accounts** used at the end of each accounting period. Class 9 is called Result Analysis and Closing Accounts. This class is used to identify and analyze all different variances and special amounts, as well as to receive three different profit and loss information.

Emanuel Schwarz

Exhibit 11-1

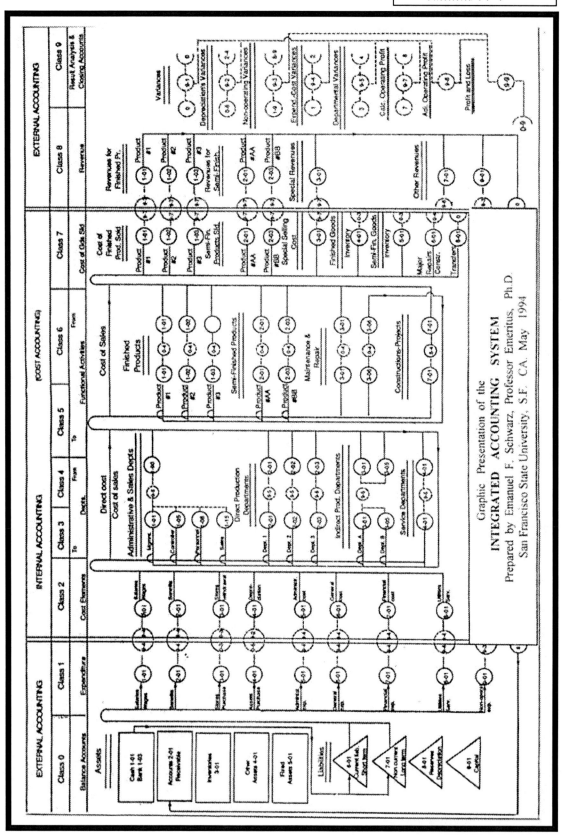

60

These ten Classes provide all the information needs for a representative and meaningful managerial accounting system. Within these ten Classes, all accounts are identified under specific Groups. This makes it easier to find and analyze the accounts. Each Class may have up to nine different Groups. These Groups are defined and identified in accordance with the specific Class.

For an easier graphical understanding of this system, the following signs and rules are used:

Assets accounts are represented by rectangles:

Liability accounts are triangles:

All other accounts are shown as circles:

Transactions from one account to another are moved along the lines that connect these circles, rectangles, or triangles. Month-end transactions move along the path of the dotted lines in this graphical presentation. Dotted line circles refer to accounts used during the month-end transactions.

Exhibit 11-2 shows some examples of how these accounts are used. In this exhibit, as is traditional, all transactions move from the credit of one account to the debit of another account, from left to right. In the same way, the movement in the whole system flows basically from left to right. Many graphs today show arrow heads at the end of the transaction lines both toward the debits and credits. This should not be done. The recording should always be from credit to debit. In the lower left corner of Exhibit 11-2, we see that two liability accounts are credited and the amount moves along the line toward two Expenditure accounts. Arrows show this transaction movement and direction. The amount moving from the lower liability account moves up along the line and turns to the right and flows down toward the two Expenditure accounts.

The basic rule of this flow indicates that NO amount is allowed in its flow upward to turn to the left. If this were permitted, that would mean it would be possible to have two credit transactions which, naturally, is contrary to the double entry procedure. Neither is it appropriate procedure to have some amount flow from the credit side of an account down the line. In a case for which this transaction is necessary, this flow is identified with a special arrow. Two special movement examples are shown in the lower right of Exhibit 11-2.

As mentioned before, dotted lines are reserved for month-end transactions. During the accounting period, all accrued invoices are charged to the different Expenditure accounts.

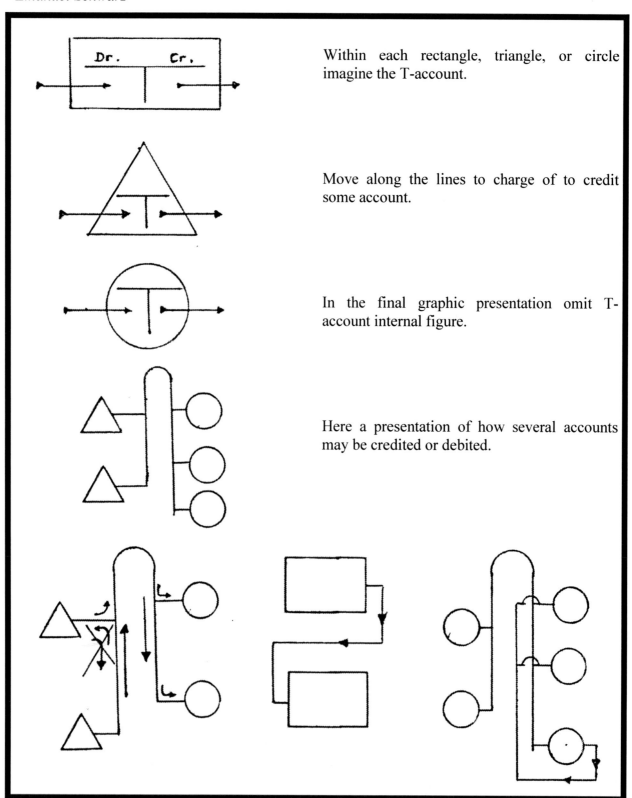

Within each rectangle, triangle, or circle imagine the T-account.

Move along the lines to charge of to credit some account.

In the final graphic presentation omit T-account internal figure.

Here a presentation of how several accounts may be credited or debited.

Exhibit 11-2: Examples of Cost-flow Patterns.

At the end of each period, it is necessary to balance these accounts by crediting them with the corresponding amount, then transferring this balance to the indicated account in Class 9 or Class 0. We will discuss the rules of the month-end closing transactions in Chapter 19.

We can see in the total graphic presentation that under Class 1 and 2 the dotted lines are moving toward dotted half circles. This is just a practical convention to avoid the need to use more space with complete circles. The same situation occurs between Classes 7 and 8.

In Class 8, the different accounts are credited and the debits moved toward the Asset accounts (accounts payable, or cash). The arrows indicate this transaction, and at the bottom of Class 8, is a half circle with a zero in its center. This is also just a way to show where these amounts will go. On the left side of the presentation is the other half of this circle with an 8 inside.

The purpose of this total graphic presentation is to make it easier to understand the system's logic flow for those who are not accountants and who must know the purpose of these accounting transactions. However, this presentation does not show all the transactions and details that may be necessary to achieve in this integrated managerial accounting.

CHAPTER 12

CODE STRUCTURE

Logically, each account must have some name or identification. For practical purposes, we prefer to use a simple code for each account. As we already discussed, the whole Integrated Accounting System is divided into ten Classes of specific types of accounts which are shown in Exhibit 11-1.

Let us now analyze Class 1:

1. Class 1 corresponds to all Expenditures that we have to register during a one month accounting period. These Expenditures represent accrued amounts and are recorded in this Class independent of whether we pay them on the same day or in the future.

2. It would not be practical to have just one Class of accounts without being able to identify these different expenditures in some appropriate Group of accounts.

3. Consequently, Class 1 is divided into nine different Groups of accounts. Names and codes are assigned for each of these groups. Group 1, for example, refers to expenditures related to Salaries and Wages.

4. Within each Group all accounts are organized under the specification of Main accounts.

5. Within Group1, Salaries and Wages, we have two specific Main accounts. One refers only to Salaries and the other Main account refers only to Wages.

    Class Group Main account
    1   1   01 Salaries.
    1   1   02 Wages.

6. Now that we have more detailed information within each Group of accounts, we know from experience that in an industry, we may have more than nine different Main accounts. Therefore, we assigned two digits to define or identify each Main account. This means that we may have up to 99 Main accounts.

7. For practical purposes, it is necessary to identify specific types of salaries or wages within each Main account. Therefore, we assigned Sub-accounts within each Main account. This structure requires a capacity of more than nine Sub-accounts. We suggest a total of three digits to open and identify each Sub-account.

Based on our extensive practical experience, we recommend incorporating a uniform code structure for the whole Integrated Accounting System. This code would have the following format:

CLASS	GROUP	MAIN ACCOUNT	SUB-ACCOUNT
X	X	XX	XXX

This indicates that each Class could have up to 9 different Groups of accounts; each Group could have up to 99 different Main accounts; and each Main account could have up to 999 Sub-accounts. This results in a numeric code of 7 digits. Under special conditions, this code could be increased by a 4 digit Detail Account (or Sub-Sub-account) which could be used for Accounts Receivable and Payable.

Let us look at this code logic more closely.

Each Class identifies its accounts with this 7digit code. The first digit starting from the left, indicates to which Class this account corresponds. It is immediately evident, therefore, whether this account belongs to the External or to the Internal Accounting. After some practical experience, we will be able to readily identify the Group to which a particular transaction belongs.

We do not recommend that a code be limited to only four digits. Our structure is designed to give a good deal of significant information. It is essential to have a working code that has many digits for your use rather than being limited by just a few. Also, we should not mix several different classes of accounts within one code. We recommend, for example, a separate code for expenditures and a separate code for departments.

Let us now analyze the following table, which gives us a detailed recommendation about code and name structure.

EXHIBIT 12-1: Code Structure Details

Class = CL Group = GR Main account = MA Sub-account = SA

<u>CL GR MA SA Denomination</u>

CL	GR	MA	SA	Denomination
1	0	00	000	<u>EXPENDITURES</u> Class name in capital letters, two underlines.
1	1	00	000	<u>SALARIES AND WAGES</u>
1	1	01	000	<u>Salaries</u> Group and Main A. written differently
1	1	01	001	Management
1	1	01	002	
1	1	01	003	
1	1	02	000	<u>Wages</u>
1	1	02	001	Direct Labor
1	1	02	002	

This is an example of a simple rollup system. The total amount of all Sub-accounts is the amount of the corresponding Main account. The total amount of several Main accounts correspond to the total amount of the Group account.

An invoice received will have to be recorded within External Accounting as well as within Internal Accounting. The following example will clarify this statement.

The invoice refers to a telephone bill. The telephone is used by the sales department. Therefore, the invoice will be credited to A/P and debited to <u>Telephone Expenditures.</u> The same amount corresponds to the expired portion for the Internal Accounting. We have to credit the <u>Telephone Cost</u> account and debit the sales department account. Graphically, the transactions are:

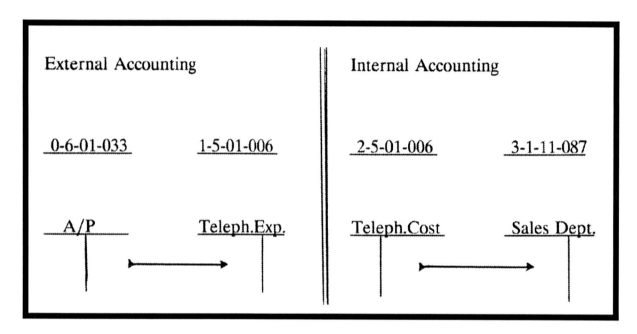

EXHIBIT 12-2: Invoice Recording

This shows us two important practical points. First, at the moment that we identify the External Accounting codes for this invoice, we also recognize the codes for the Internal Accounting. Second, we can also see that the telephone code in the External side guides us to establish the code in the Internal. These two Classes have identical codes with the exception of the first digit: 1 for Expenditures Class and 2 for Cost Element Class. The whole code structure is simple, straightforward, and logical!

In Exhibit 1-22, we show all four codes. This is just a guide. A good software program will be designed with pre-established space for these four Classes, will reduce work to a minimum, and will provide maximum information.

DEPARTMENT CODE STRUCTURE

The code of individual departments is precise and accurate when expressed with a seven digit code. As can be seen in the total graphic presentation, there are four basic groups of departments. These Groups are:

Group 1 : ADMINISTRATIVE and SALES DEPARTMENT

Group 2 : DIRECT PRODUCTION DEPARTMENT

Group 3 : INDIRECT PRODUCTION DEPARTMENT

Group 4: SERVICE DEPARTMENT

Within each Group there are several Main accounts identifying the different departments; within each department, there are several cost centers. In setting up a code system, it is advisable, <u>not</u> to use totally consecutive numbers in the code structure, since it is more practical to leave some blank spaces for numbers that might be necessary to use in the future when new accounts need to be added. For example, let us analyze the following table:

Department :	3	1	01	001	name		
	3	1	01	002	of		
	3	1	01	003		specific	
	3	1	01	004			centers.

It is better to identify the specific centers with a Sub-account code and to leave room to include new accounts as follows:

Department:	3	1	01	001	name		
	3	1	01	003	of		
	3	1	01	007		specific	
	3	1	01	011			centers.

We use the same structure with Main accounts.

After the cost centers are recorded in the first Main account, we need to leave room for future use of Main accounts. The whole code structure will be more flexible:

First	3	1	01	001	Second	3	1	05	001
Department	3	1	01	004	Department	3	1	05	003
	3	1	01	007		3	1	05	006

A closer look into the structure of the code reveals the following possibility: If it is necessary or desirable, we may use the first digit to the left of the Main account for some basic information, and the second digit can be used as a detailed structure of this information. For example:

3	2	30	000	Direct Production Department: Workshops
3	2	31	000	Workshop A
3	2	33	000	Workshop B

The operating cost of these two workshops fall under the Workshop Main account 3-2-30-000.

This same approach can be used with the three digits of the Sub-account number. The first digit to the left identifies some general description of the Sub-account and the next two digits are then related to a more specific identification of this Sub-account. The department is identified with the first digit to the left, and the different cost centers of this department are specified by the last two digits of the Sub-account code.

Let us here reiterate some important points related to the basic code structure of this system:

CLASS 0: This Class contains all accounts related to the Balance. Adding and subtracting all accounts under Class code 0 results in accurate and useful information about balancing assets and liabilities.

CLASS 1 and 2: These Classes are interrelated closely. With the exception of Group 9 of these Classes, all other Groups in these two Classes have a corresponding nomenclature or corresponding description of the expired portion of expenditure. The Store Purchase Group in Class 1 corresponds to Stores Withdrawal Group in Class 2, and Assets Purchases correspond to Depreciation in Class 2.

CLASS 3 and 4: These are interrelated and coordinated in their code structure which is a natural and logical consequence.

CLASS 5 and 6: These are interrelated and coordinated in their code structure.

CLASS 7 and 8: These are largely designed to be code coordinated. There are, however, some Groups of accounts in Class 7 that are not represented in Class 8.

Within the rectangles, triangles, and circles in the graphic presentation of the Integrated System, a number identifies the Group of accounts along with the next two numbers related to the Main account. This is not the case with the numbers within the dotted line circles. In these cases, it is necessary to indicate both the Class of accounts to which the balance will be transferred and also the corresponding Group, as shown in Exhibit 1-23.

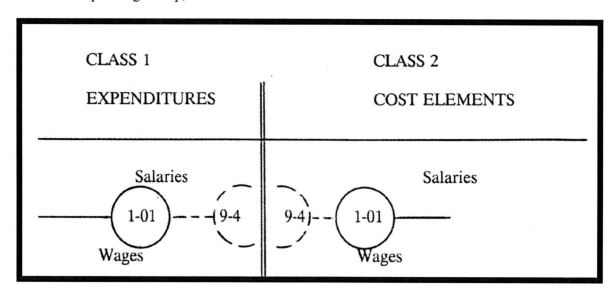

EXHIBIT 12-3: Identification of Accounts.

A PRACTICAL OBSERVATION

From a practical point of view, we suggest that a Main account or Sub-account never begin with the code 00/000. It is necessary to recognize that the first number in a series starts with the number 1 and not with 0. The number 0 follows after the number 9 and will be complemented by the number 1 in front of it.

As an example, we may develop the following:

COST ELEMENTS:

2	1	00	000	Group of Accounts
2	1	00	000	is <u>not</u> the code of a Main account
2	1	01	000	is the first Main account
2	1	01	000	is <u>not</u> the first Sub-account
2	1	01	001	is the first Sub-account.

CHAPTER 13

STORES INVENTORY
TRANSACTIONS

One of the most interesting and complicated accounts is the Stores Inventory, which is why it is also very important to understand in detail. When it is clearly understood how this particular account is used, along with the purposes of its different Sub-accounts, it will also be easier to understand the whole philosophy and value of the Integrated Accounting System and its concepts of separate and distinct accounts. Let us, then, take an in-depth look at the Inventory Stores account.

Exhibit 13-1 shows how today's inventory account is used and how our Integrated System transforms this account into several individual steps that have their specific meaning and purpose. In the upper part of this exhibit is the "traditional" way of using the Inventory Stores account. Only one Inventory Stores account exists (as part of the Assets) and in this account is recorded the Beginning Balance (b.b.), to which is added all purchases in the debit column; all purchase returned to vendor are recorded in the credit column. Also, in the credit column, all withdrawals are accounted for. Any returns of withdrawals will also be debited to this account.

To use a specific example, let us assume that it is a Raw Material Inventory account. Let us further suppose that there is a perpetual inventory control and that every month there is a physical check of several items (we would not, in reality, check all items every month). This means that there may be some inventory adjustments each month. If there are more raw materials than expected, this amount is identified as "gain" in the debit column; if there is less raw material than expected, this is identified as "loss" in the credit column. At the end of the period, the ending Balance (e.b.) of this account is developed. All inventory stores transactions are always related to this one account, even if we also use some subsidiary ledgers.

The Integrated Accounting System divides the purchase and withdrawal transactions into two specific accounts:

PURCHASE is recorded as an Expenditure, and in this system it is debited to Stores Purchase in Class 1.

WITHDRAWAL is the amount related to the expired portion of the Stores Purchase; this amount is accurately accounted for and appropriately allocated in the Internal Accounting structure. Accountants will quickly observe that under today's system a purchase of raw material is accumulated directly into an asset account - a credit directly to Accounts Payable and a direct debit to the corresponding Inventory Stores account. This observation is reasonable when we have an accounting system that does not have a special expenditure class.

But not all purchases are that simple to allocate. Let us look at an example that can raise some questions.

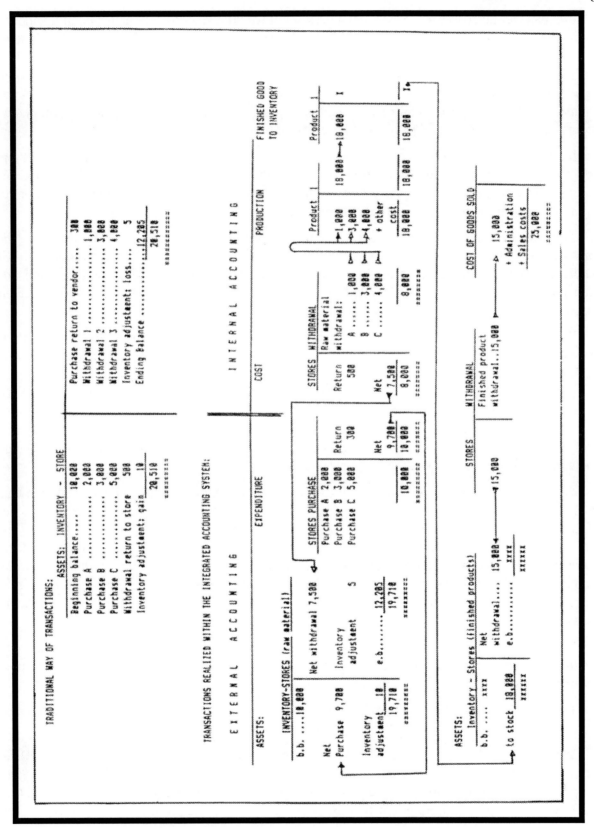

EXHIBIT 13-1: Graphic of Inventory Transactions.

If a manager purchases a $75.00 special desk set, it would be recorded as an expenditure and the entire amount would also be charged as a cost for this accounting period. We know that this desk set will probably be in the office of the manager for many years, so it could be reasoned that this desk set is a part of the assets. This is almost never done, however, because it is usually determined not to be worthwhile or not to be cost effective. If something is purchased that will still be in the company's possession at the end of an accounting period, and if it is worthwhile to identify and designate this purchase, it will be recorded in some Asset account.

If we accept this accounting procedure enough to follow it, we consequently have to accept that any purchase is an expenditure of the company. At the end of the accounting period when this purchase was realized, it becomes necessary to acknowledge, analyze, and determine whether or not a purchase will be recorded as part of the Assets.

Through the preceding example, it becomes easier to understand the logic behind the transactions that are used for the Stores Inventory accounts in the Integrated Accounting. All purchases would be recorded in the Stores Purchase account in Class 1: Expenditures, and any return of such purchases are to be credited to this same account. This purchase transaction (accrued amount) is part of today's or the future's cash outflow.

We can clearly see this first step by recording the amount of the purchase in our Exhibit 13-1. We charge all purchases to the Expenditure account of Stores Purchase (Class 1). The credit of these amounts are not recorded in this graphic exhibit because of insufficient space. The credit would be registered in the A/P. In the credit of the Expenditure account (Class 1), we have identified the amount of purchase returns to our vendors. We can see that this account is a so-called "pure" account; that is, we do not mix purchases with withdrawals in the same account. Recall that Professor Horngren established two Department accounts: one to which is charted the actual value and another to which is credited the absorbed amount.

All store's withdrawals correspond to Internal Accounting. Consequently, all source documents referring to withdrawals are recorded in Internal Accounting. The amount of raw material taken out of inventory for use in production is credited in Class 2, Stores Withdrawal, as a Cost Element for this period. This is a classic example of an expired portion of Expenditure. We recorded first the accrued amount in Class 1, Stores Purchases, then we used this purchase in our production and the amount we took out of the Inventory is just the expired portion for this accounting period. From Stores Withdrawal, this raw material amount is to be charged to the Production Cost account in Class 5.

If we have return of some raw material from production to Inventory, the amount returned will require the same procedure but in the opposite direction. Thus, we would credit this returned amount in Class 5 and debit it in Class 2.

This recording constitutes an exception from the normal rule that Class 2 should only be credited and class 5 only debited.

We can see in Exhibit 13-1 that when we finish this Job order, we transfer the raw material amount (along with other cost elements) from Class 6 to Class 7, Finished Goods Inventory. Here we presume that the Job order was started and finished in the same accounting period, and that no partial transfer was made from production to inventory.

At the end of each accounting period, the balance of each of these accounts Purchase, Withdrawal, and Finished Goods Inventory is transferred to the corresponding Asset Inventory account.

As we can see in Exhibit 13-1, the net purchase amount in the Class 1 account of Stores Purchase is credited in this account and transferred to the debit of the Asset account of Inventory Stores (raw material). This means that the beginning balance which we had in this account will be increased with the net purchase amount.

The next step is to balance the Class 2 account of Stores Withdrawal and debit this account with the net withdrawal amount and transfer it to the credit of the Asset Inventory Stores account. This whole procedure is a logical and practical one because we have pure accounts through which we may control the total purchase and total withdrawal, plus have an Inventory Stores account that is also simple to control.

In Exhibit 13-1, we also have the Finished Goods Inventory account in our Internal Accounting. This account is, as we already mentioned, a contra account. At the end of each month we have to transfer the balance from this account to the External Accounting's Finished Goods Inventory account.

An interesting point in our Integrated Accounting System is that, during the accounting period, we do not use the Inventory Stores account in the Assets. In the beginning of the period, this account will receive the amount of the beginning balance, then stay untouched. Toward the end of the month, we use this account to record the net purchase and withdrawal amounts. Only the inventory adjustments will be recorded on this Asset account because they are really Asset adjustments.

Next, a relatively simple step in the natural movement of products is the sales transaction of these finished goods. First we have to prepare a Store's Withdrawal source document. The amount of this document will be credited in Class 2 as Stores Withdrawal of Finished Goods. This amount will be allocated to Class 7, Cost of Goods Sold.

At the end of each month we proceed in the same way as we did with raw material transactions: The net amount of Finished Goods Withdrawal is debited to the Class 2 account and then credited to the Inventory account in the Assets. Note that the amount recorded in Class 7 is not to be taken back to Assets, but to be transferred to the Income Summary account.

This transaction is discussed in Chapter 19.

STANDARD COSTS FOR RAW MATERIAL

If management wishes to introduce Standard Cost for raw material, the following procedure is useful:

1. The inventory of raw material in the Store (Assets) should be recorded at actual price. We would not recommend, however, registering the raw material inventory account at standard cost. The price variance should not refer to the total purchased amount. This purchased amount could be relatively large because most stores buy for some time ahead. Note that the Just in Time theory requires purchasing the amount that we need just for this moment. In our opinion, it is more logical to show the price variance each month referring to the quantity used during that month, in the same way that we show it with Payment Variance in the Direct Labor account. The Purchasing department will have to inform Accounting of any price variance that may have resulted between the standard price (budgeted) and the

actual price that came to be registered in the invoice of the vendor. Admittedly, this is a matter of choice.

2. In Class 2, we have the Stores Withdrawal account. From this account, we move the actual quantity, times actual price amount, to the Price Variance account. We need to establish this account within Class 2 in the same Group 3 where all Withdrawals appear, but we use the higher code number of the Main account.

3. In this Price Variance account we credit the amount that we would receive by multiplying the actual quantity, times standard price. If we receive a difference between debit and credit amounts, this difference refers to the Price Variance.

4. From the credit of the Price Variance account, we need to transfer the amount to the debit of the Efficiency account. We then compare this amount with the value of the raw material standard quantity, times the standard price. The standard quantity must refer to the Good Output of production during this accounting period. That is, it refers to the actual, finished production of the month, and not to the budgeted quantity that we prepared in the beginning of the year.

The graphic presentation of this is shown in Exhibit 13-2.

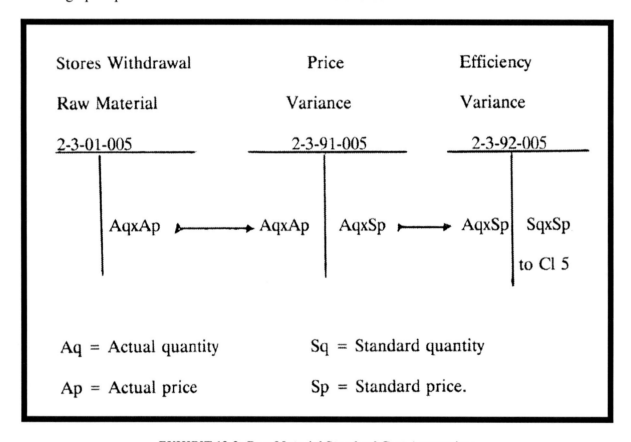

EXHIBIT 13-2: Raw Material Standard Cost Accounting.

CHAPTER 14

DIRECT LABOR TRANSACTIONS

To record and determine the Direct Labor payroll, the following system would be quite logical.

EXTERNAL ACCOUNTING:

Credit: Accounts Payable Payroll

Debit : Expenditure Direct Labor wages

In Accounts Payable, it is possible to use one general descriptive account without identifying the salaries or wages. In class 1, a Main account is used, developed especially for the Direct Labor wages. Payroll structured by departments would identify which employees are earning a direct labor wage. This is a pre-established condition to be changed only if the supervisor of the employee provides necessary information.

INTERNAL ACCOUNTING:

Credit : Cost Elements Direct Labor wages.

Debit : Direct Production Department.

Normally, Class 2 has the same amount of direct labor wages as Class 1. If a calendar month period is used, however, the expired portion of the expenditure may differ for the last week of payment because several days of this wage payment belong to one period   and the other days belong to the next period. Nevertheless, in Class 2, the total payment is realized as direct labor. Class 3 naturally   receives the transferred amount, which corresponds to each of the   Direct Production Departments.

It would be appropriate here to answer a question that always comes up during a discussion of labor costs analysis: Is direct labor a variable cost?

The answer must be:

YES, if the wages are paid per unit of production.

NO, if the wages are paid per hour.

This answer is based following the very basic rule that defines variable and fixed costs when determining production cost:

Variable costs will change proportionally to changes in production activity level.

If the direct labor wages are paid per hour of production, and actual production activity level drops with 5%, that means that we have produced not 100 units per hour, but only 95 units, yet the same total wages would be paid.

If we charge to the 95 units produced the actual wages paid, the result is a higher unit production cost. It is correct to establish that the unit cost increased because we had lower labor efficiency. But if we do not have a special account which shows this labor efficiency variance (comparing actual labor time used with the budgeted time), we have no way of knowing why the unit cost of the production increased this month and/or for this job order. To get the necessary control with adequate detailed information, we have to enter the Standard Labor cost procedure.

Let us clarify here some other details. Each Direct Production department has a predetermined number of Direct Labor employees related to the established Direct Labor budget for this department. It is appropriate to charge to the corresponding Direct Production department the actual Direct Labor wages paid, and, of course, compare this amount with the budgeted value. It is clear that for responsible cost control, Direct Labor wages should always be charged to a Direct Production department. This procedure is the reason we do <u>not</u> allocate Direct Labor costs directly to a Class 5, Production Cost account. Clearly, a more accurate internal accounting requires the transfer of the actual Direct Labor paid to the Direct Production department.

This is a very important and new approach.

Let us not transfer Direct Labor wages from credit Payroll account to debit Production Cost account (or as it is called today Work In Process), but charge these wages to the corresponding Direct Production Departments.

The following important changes become necessary:

1. That we stop using the term "Overhead" and identify these accounts as related to all departments of our company;

2. That we charge Direct Labor wages to the corresponding Direct Production departments;

3. We recommend using multiple absorption rates for each Direct Production department, certainly not one rate for all departments.

Exhibit 14-1 clearly demonstrates the preceding concepts:

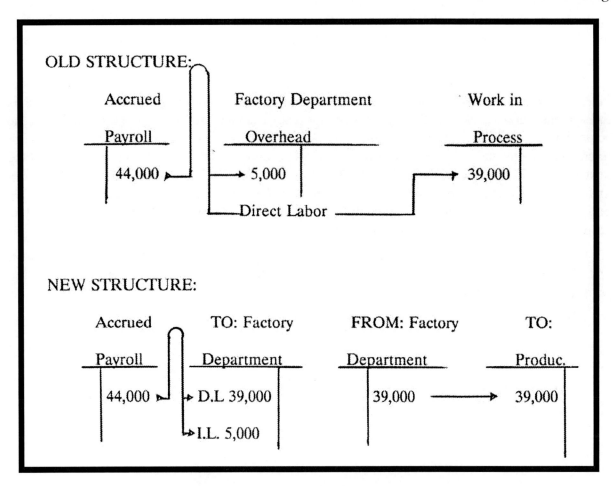

EXHIBIT 14-1; Direct Labor recording procedure.

Exhibit 14-1 shows us that today Direct Labor wages are not identified as a Factory Department cost.

They are transferred directly to the Work in Process account. The Indirect Labor Wages are recognized as a cost related to the Factory Department. This method of recording labor wages gives the impression that the direct labor is not part of the Factory Department, which is clearly not correct. Both the direct labor and the indirect labor come under the same Factory Department. And both the wages for the direct labor as well as the indirect labor are included in the budget of this factory department.

As we mentioned before, the term, "Overhead," should be totally excluded from modern cost accounting terminology, as lacking in true accountability.

STANDARD COST FOR DIRECT LABOR

It may become desirable to charge to the Production Cost account, the Direct Labor wages expressed in standard time and standard payments. This is done the same way as was done for developing a standard cost for raw material, described in the preceding chapter.

As mentioned before, it is necessary to charge the Direct Production departments of Class 3 the actual wages paid, which is the consequence of multiplying the actual hours times the actual payment. we now need to create two new accounts which will show us the two variances related to the Direct Wages. The first account refers to Payment Variances, and the second account refers to Efficiency Variance.

These two new accounts make it necessary to credit the Direct Production department's account in Class 4, with the actual payment and transfer of this amount to the first variance account, which is to Payment Variance. We credit this Payment Variance account with the amount that refers to the actual hours, times the standard payment. Any difference between debit and credit in this account refers to the Payment Variance. By crediting this last account, we take the amount to the debit of the next account which refers to the Efficiency Variance. The last step is to establish the standard hours that employees should have used to produce the Good Output. This Good Output refers to the budgeted production volume or to some other amount which happened to be produced during this accounting period. Recall that we have to control this Good Output monthly.

Once we have the standard hours for the Good Output, we multiply it by the standard payment, and the total amount is credited to this Efficiency Variance account and absorbed by the corresponding Production Cost accounts.

This is shown graphically in Exhibit 14-2.

The variances which we receive in these accounts may be transferred to a Variance summary account in Class 9, or directly to the Adjusted Operating Profit in this same Class 9.

We recommend the Variance summary account.

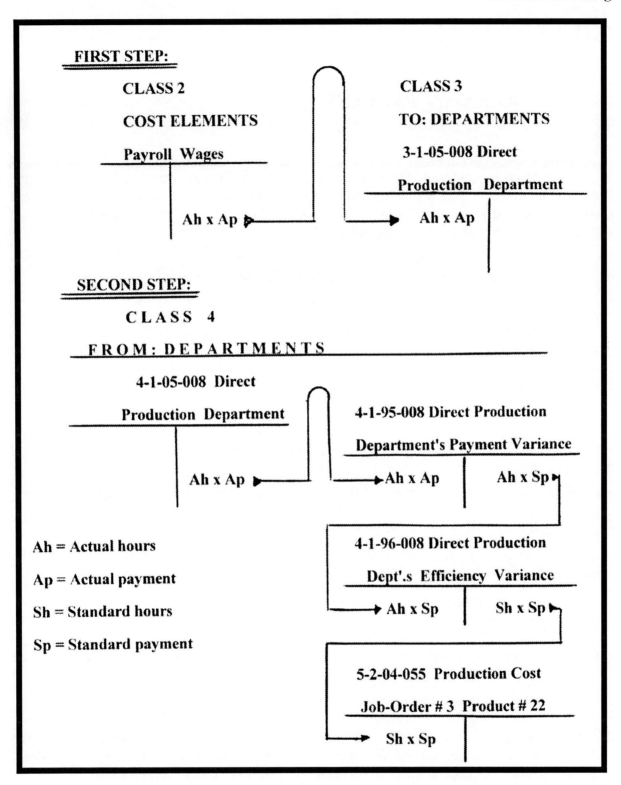

EXHIBIT 14-2: Standard Direct Labor Wage's recording.

CHAPTER 15

WORK IN PROCESS

If there is no separation of the Financial Accounting (External) from the Cost Accounting (Internal), it becomes necessary to use the description of "Work-in-Process Inventory" for the account that is used to identify the cost of production. This "Work in Process Inventory" account will naturally be a part of the Assets accounts.

And this structure in our present cost accounting where we identify Work-in-Process (WIP) as an inventory account has created the greatest confusion in modern teaching of cost accounting.

It is essential to define the following terminology basic to accounting:

WORK-IN-PROCESS: refers to the difference between the debit and the credit amounts. A glossary would identify Work in Process as an uncompleted work off the production on the production line. And so should it be taken. We should not refer to debited amounts as Work in Process. This creates an incorrect and inaccurate concept and this is just what happened in teaching cost accounting.

WORK-IN-PROCESS: is a balance amount; that is, it refers to the amount of uncompleted work that the factory had in its different direct production departments at the moment the monthly records are closed.

The next working day this amount of WIP will change within a short time because of the new activity. Consequently, we should not talk of "Total cost of Work-in-Process for the year," as we do not say "Total ending inventory of raw material for the year."

The following is a typical inaccurate example taken from COST ACCOUNTING , written by Professors Edward B. Deakin and Michael W. Maher, 2nd Edition 1987, page 27:

"... the Work in Process Inventory account had a beginning balance on January 1 of $ 580,00. Costs incurred during the year were $1,640,000 in direct material ...; $3,240,000 in direct labor costs; and $2,850,000 in overhead. The $7,730,000 sum of these last three items is the cost of manufacturing incurred during the year. Adding the beginning work in process inventory to the $7,730,000 gives the TOTAL COST OF WORK IN PROCESS FOR THE YEAR."

We must emphasize that there cannot be a Work-in-Process amount for the year. We have to refer to this amount as the total manufacturing cost during the year. The basic confusion arose when this manufacturing cost account, WIP, was created in External Accounting within the Assets. The only clear solution is to separate the WIP inventory account from the manufacturing cost account. This separation of Internal and External accounting, as we have clearly demonstrated, provides us with an ideal solution:

1. A special Production Cost (Manufacturing cost) account should be created in the Internal Accounting and is NOT to be identified as Work in Process. It will be within Class 5, which refers to the production activity with all necessary Main accounts and Sub-accounts

for the different products that we manufacture. This account belongs to the production activity of the month and consequently does NOT have any beginning or ending balance.

2. An inventory account of what was in process at the moment of closing the monthly activity will be created within the Asset accounts. This Working Process account has the beginning balance to which we add the production cost of the month (we may naturally control it by products and by Job Orders) and credit this account with the good output production of the month. The difference between debit and credit will be the Work in Process at the end of the month.

Exhibit 15-1 shows graphically the relationship between product cost and the Work-in-Process account.

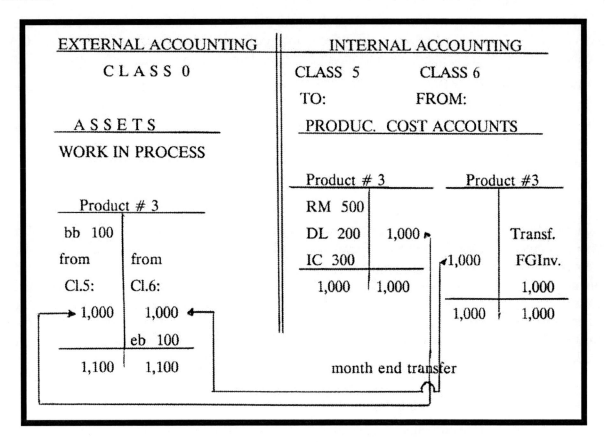

EXHIBIT 15-1: **Product Cost and Work-in-Process Accounts.**

In the Internal Accounting system, we have created two production cost accounts for Product #3: one in Class 5 to which we debit the cost of the month (or of the Job order), and one in Class 6 from which we transfer the good output of the month to the Finished Goods Inventory account in Class 7.

The accounts of Class 5 and Class 6 are the working accounts for internal managerial information. These accounts do not appear as any other account within the Internal Accounting, in the Balance Sheet, or in the Income Statement. At the end of each accounting period (or when any

Job order is finished), it is important to transfer the amounts accumulated on these accounts to the Work-in-Process, Product #3 account in the Assets. This WIP account contains beginning and ending balances for this particular Job order. If production is a continuous flow process, beginning and ending balances will be nearly the same amount, whether there is a delay in the transfer of finished goods to the Finished Goods Inventory, or whether some other unforeseen factor, makes the ending balance of work in process different from the beginning balance. Only if we have a Job order production that normally covers a several month period, will the beginning and ending balance amounts of Work-in-Process show great differences.

With Job order production, we actually are NOT interested in the ending or beginning balances. We are interested in the control of the Job order itself: How much did this Job order actually cost us compared with the standard values. But the amount that was at the end of a particular month in process of Job order production is of little importance.

During the month, we may have several Job orders finished; the production cost of each of these orders is of real interest to management. These Job orders are recorded in the Production Cost accounts of Class 5 and 6, but these costs have nothing to do with the work in process values.

Let us remember that Class 5 and Class 6 refer not only to the manufacturing process, but also to these Job orders that control repairs and internal production. Repair orders may last longer than one accounting period; and at the end of the first period, the Work-in-Process amount may correspond to the total cost invested in repair during the first period.

Repair will be completed during the second month and its total amount will be credited to the corresponding account in Cl.6 and transferred to Cl.7.

When we record our own construction of a machine or a building, we have to credit Class 6 each month with the same amount as we have charged Class 5 of this construction. We will not have any amount in Work-in-Process, because we will have to open a special "In Construction" account in some corresponding Assets group. The total amount of what we have invested during this month in this construction will be transferred from Class 6 to Class 7. From this account in Class 7 we allocate this amount to the "In Construction" in Class 0 Assets. This account accumulates monthly amounts, which are investments in this construction, and when we have finished this project, the total amount is then recorded in corresponding Assets accounts. The structure of our Internal Accounting and its corresponding terminology are as follows:

Class 3 will have the cost that we allocate to the Direct Production Departments (and other departments);

Class 5 will have the cost allocated to and absorbed by the different products.

Consequently, we should not mix the flow of costs to the departments with those of the production cost accounts. We avoid statements such as:

"... the manufacturing costs that were charged to the two departments are as follows:

		Assembly	Finished
Direct Material.		$ xxx	0
Direct Labor.		$ xxx	$ xxxx
Manufacturing OH.		$ xxx	$ xxxx
	Totals	$ xxx	$ xxxx

Let us clarify this concept. The production departments were not charged with the Direct Material. This Direct Material was allocated to the Production Cost accounts (today called Work-in-Process).

Here again we can see the basic current misunderstanding of what is Internal Accounting's cost flow. The correct Internal Accounting Cost-flow procedure is as follows:

1. ALLOCATE the direct production costs to the Product Cost accounts. Direct material will not be allocated to Departments.

2. ALLOCATE the indirect production costs to the departments. In our example, the company should have two direct production departments: Assembly and Finishing. We charge both Direct Labor and all other departmental operating costs to these accounts.

3. ABSORPTION of Direct Labor and departmental operating costs by the production. This absorption will be separately realized for the Direct Labor cost, and absorption rates are used to transfer the departmental operating costs.

Let us analyze Exhibit 15-2, which is Prof. E.B. Deakin's illustration taken from his Cost Accounting book:

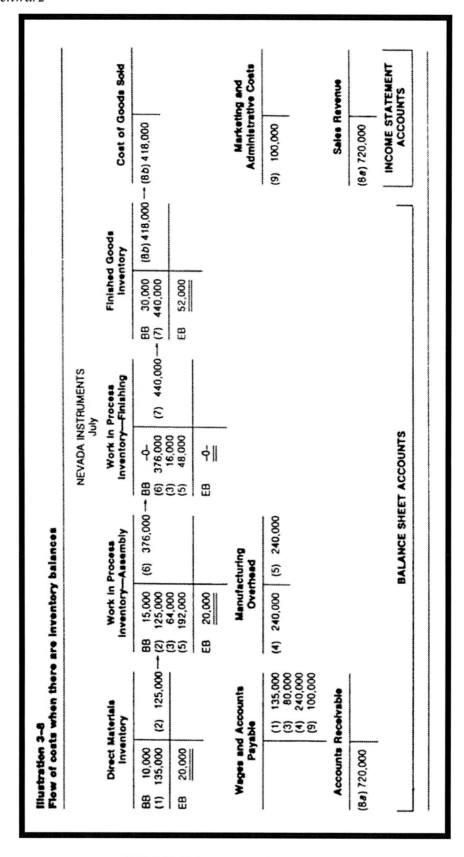

EXHIBIT 15-2: Analysis of Flow of Costs

This exhibit refers to a factory with two production departments: Assembly and Finishing. It produces only one product. As we can see, there are two Work-in-Process Inventory accounts: one for the assembly activity and the other for the finishing activity.

They should be identified as something other than the two abovementioned departments, and therefore it is incorrect to say:

.. manufacturing costs that were charged to the two departments are ... Direct materials." In no way should we indicate that Direct Material was charged to the departments. These WIP are the functional activity accounts, or simply, production cost accounts (manufacturing cost).

We also observe that Exhibit 15-2 contains only ONE manufacturing Overhead account (Direct Production Department), but the information we received indicates that the factory has two departments.

This observation is of deep significance, because it has created in our minds the idea that we should have only ONE overhead account. Today's practical experience shows that there are over 50% of the medium sized industries that use only one overhead account and, consequently, only one absorption rate for all their production departments.

We strongly recommend that the term Overhead be replaced by a term that identifies this account with the name of a specific direct production department, or simply mention that it is a department. Exhibit 15-2 requires that we show there are two production departments, just as there are two activities that management wishes to control.

Professor Deakin's book gives the following statement regarding the accounting transactions in Exhibit 15-2: item (3) refers "... to record costs of direct labor work in each manufacturing department". These amounts are not allocated to the departments, but charged directly to the WIP accounts. This is a confusing situation, and a new and more clear procedure should be adapted.

We have already established that the factory has only one product. Consequently, the Direct Labor wages charged to the WIP Inv. Assembly account correspond to the wages of this Assembly department. But if the factory has several different products and has worked with Job orders, the control situation for responsibility accounting for different departments becomes difficult. We recommend that the Direct Labor wages be <u>allocated</u> to the corresponding Direct Production Departments, and then <u>absorbed</u> by the different Job orders. The Production Cost groups (which are today called Work-in-Process Inventory) have accounts identified with the name of products and Job order number. Names of production departments are excluded in these accounts.

The text accompanying Exhibit 15-2 tells us that the WIP and the Manufacturing Overhead accounts correspond to the Balance sheet accounts. A new confusion appears: we know that the Overhead account does NOT appear in the Balance sheet. Neither does it correspond to the Income statement. We find no other solution than to include in this illustration, the Overhead account as part of the Balance sheet accounts. This confirms our statements in the beginning of this book that the Financial Accounting should not cover Internal Accounting. The frame prepared for the Financial Accounting is not designed to include the Internal Accounting needs and necessities.

Exhibit 15-3 is the new illustration of flow of costs.

We would like to call the reader's attention to the following detail in the Exhibit 15-2 that is also confusing:

The WIP Inventory account has a beginning balance (BB) recorded in the debit. On the same debit side is also recorded the ending balance (EB).

This is not a meaningful presentation, since the ending balance is the difference between the total amount in debit and credit. Then in these inventory accounts, the debit is normally larger than the credit, and consequently the ending balance has to be recorded on the credit side. As these amounts are indicated as ending balance, they have to be on the credit side. To record them on the debit side means that these amounts must refer to the beginning balance. This is a widespread practice not only in cost accounting books, but also in principles of accounting texts.

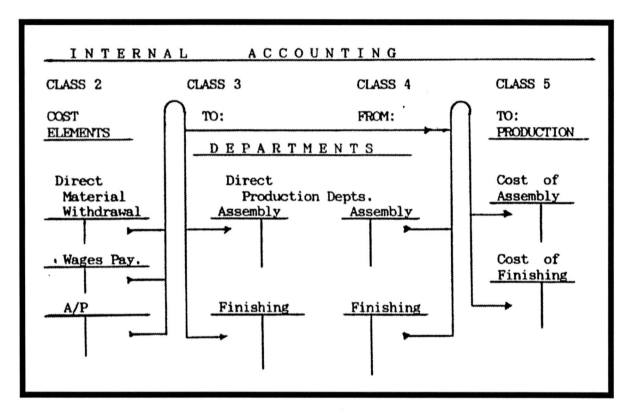

EXHIBIT 15-3: Illustration of Flow of Costs.

A PRACTICAL EXAMPLE.

Let us evaluate, using our new method, the Work-in-Process account in our Assets. We can begin our production activity in January with a zero beginning balance of Work-in-Process, and refer to this account as 0401001. A simplified model for this is shown in Exhibit 15-4.

During the production cycle of this monthly ac counting period we charge the Production Cost account 5101001 with the value of raw material, direct labor, and departmental operating costs. The total amount is $40. These are standard production costs, and it is known that the standard unit cost is $4.00 The finished goods inventory has accepted a total of 9 units during this period. That is the good output quantity for this period. The standard production cost of this transfer is established, account 6101001 is credited, and a corresponding account in Class 7 is debited.

At the end of this month, all accounts must be balanced, including class 5 and Class 6 accounts.

Because the difference between what is introduced TO: production and what is transferred FROM production is a part of the Assets, it is necessary to transfer the balance amounts of these two accounts in Class 5 and 6 to the corresponding Asset, which is the Work-in-Process Inventory account.

In the debit column of this Work-in-Process ac count 0401001, is $40.00, the amount allocated to production; in the credit column is $36.00 as the standard cost of good output transferred to finished goods inventory. The difference ($4.00) is the amount of the Work-in-Process at the end of this period. This amount of $4.00 is just as if a photo were taken at the closing hour of the last working day of the period, the moment when the employees completed their shifts. The next working day, the whole situation will change. And what was in process will be finished products, and new amounts will be in process.

The $4.00 of Work-in-Process becomes the beginning balance for the next period, and there will be new charges to the Production Cost account for the new values of raw material, direct labor, and departmental operating costs. Let us assume that during this new accounting period the same amount is charged to the Class 5 account as was charged the month before. At the end of this second production month, a total of 10 units, at the standard cost of $ 40.00, are transferred to the Finished Goods Inventory. The second month will have a larger good output than the first month of production as a consequence of having had one unit in process. This unit will be finished in the second month and, out of the 10 new units started, 9 units (the same amount as during the first month), will be finished and transferred to the Finished Goods Inventory.

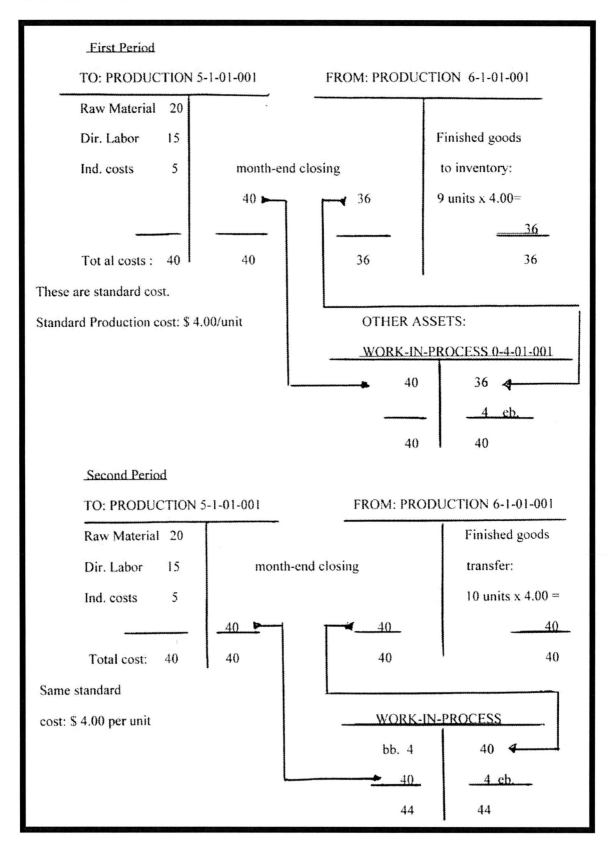

EXHIBIT 15- 4: Work-in-Process Accountability.

At the end of this month accounts are closed and the corresponding amounts are transferred to the Work-in-Process account. In WIP accounts, the debit columns have the amount of the beginning balance plus the amount of dollars charged to production ($40.00). In the credit column is the amount of finished goods transferred to inventory. Naturally, the ending balance will be the same amount as at the end of the first period.

Work-in-Process accounts in the assets can also relate to some specific Job order in production that requires special control or information.

JOB ORDERS OR PROCESS COSTING

If the production is controlled by Job orders, our interest is focused upon the actual cost contra standard one and actual time of production of this order contra standard time. It is of no interest if this order started and finished during the same calendar month, or if it is finished in next month. We need not know the amount of unfinished production of this order (Work-in-Process) the minute an accounting period was finished. The different variance accounts, however, are of interest, especially Price and Efficiency Variances of both raw material and direct labor. These variance accounts must be controlled by each Job order.

If the production is controlled by Process Costing, the whole situation is more complicated and indefinite. Only if we have the <u>same type</u> of production during the whole fiscal year or continuing during several months, would it be necessary to use Process Costing. Let us be clear that Process Costing refers to a Job order that continues for a 12month period. The correct control of how much this production actually cost is known only when we finish this order. We may then compare the actual cost with the known standard. During this long period, we have no opportunity to establish the actual production cost for only one month of our activity. The information we receive from the supervisor of the production about the percentage of production completed, is probably highly uncertain.

It is important that we understand that actually only few industries may use Process Costing, those that have only one type of product: Soya bean oil, etc. All other industries need to have Job order costing and include standard value in their costing.

CHAPTER 16

THE MAINTENANCE AND REPAIR ACCOUNTS

One important cost accounting functional activity is related to maintenance and repair costs. There is no way to responsibly avoid accountability for these types of activities. Many people are involved with these functions, so it is logical and appropriate to prepare some specific accounts which provide the necessary control and cost information.

Current accounting structures do not include such accounts, as has been shown in exhibit 2-1. Students who study these present cost-flow structures do not receive any hint about basic needs to control maintenance and repair costs. The lack of this type of instruction in our present cost-flow system has its origin in the difficult task of showing these accounts clearly within the Financial Accounting structure. This is the same problem we discussed in a previous chapter where we saw that the present cost-flow frame is good for the External Accounting but insufficient for the Internal Accounting.

In the Integrated Accounting System, we can see the group of departments related to indirect production activities. It is much easier to accept that repair and maintenance departments belong to this group.

Furthermore, the new cost-flow graph shows specific accounts to control the cost of maintenance and repair. These accounts are located within Class 5, which controls the different functional activities of the industry. Within the Internal accounting cost-flow, we have the necessary space and structure to identify and show these accounts.

THE MAINTENANCE DEPARTMENT

Some companies will not need to have separate maintenance and repair departments. They merely create one unit for these two activities. Some will have to control several departments within both maintenance and repair units. The new Chart of Accounts has the necessary capacity to give all the details that management needs. Maintenance and repair units should be opened with the Indirect Production Departments group of accounts in Class 3.

All operating costs related to these departments will be allocated to them: the salary of the supervisor, the wages earned by employees, rent, depreciation, phones, office supplies, and all general material needed to maintain or repair the buildings, the machines or vehicles. This general material refers to such supplies as grease, oil, nails, screws, bolts, nuts, paint, etc. all supplies that maintenance crews need for their daily work.

It is not always easy to separate maintenance work from repair work. Sometimes it is a question of personal opinion to identify some work as a repair and another as maintenance. Yet, within an industrial entity a separation must be done between these two activities, because maintenance may have a clearly established and evaluated budget. The industry may have special crews that are in charge of keeping the machines in good shape so the production will run smoothly and the product will be of good quality.

Maintenance activity will not have some "direct" material that would be possible to identify with some specific maintenance work.

No direct cost is allocated to the Functional Activity accounts in Class 5 for maintenance. These maintenance accounts have to absorb all operating costs of the maintenance department in Class 3. The absorption transactions will naturally be realized from Class 4 to Class 5.

Some companies will need identification of specific maintenance activities, such as buildings, machines, and vehicles. The maintenance crews will have to give the necessary information about their time spent in these functions. The total absorbed amounts during a specific month will have to be reallocated to the different departments which used these services. For example, in the maintenance of machines, the accumulated cost in Class 5 will have to be reallocated to the Direct Production departments in Class 3. We credit Class 6 and debit Class 3 accounts. The purpose for this is that these maintenance costs should become part of the operating costs of the Direct Production departments. Through the absorption rate system used with the Direct Production departments, these maintenance costs finally can be charged to the different Job orders. If management decides to receive special information on the maintenance of an important machine, these maintenance costs will have to be reallocated from Class 6 to the Job orders produced by this machine and recorded in Class 5.

We know it is not always easy to reallocate building maintenance costs. One way to do this would be to transfer these total costs to the General Management account in Class 3 if no further interest exists to reallocate them to different departments. The maintenance of vehicles could be handled in the same way.

THE REPAIR DEPARTMENT

Repair costs are more interesting in their analysis. The departmental operating costs are allocated to the department account in Class 3in the same way as we described it with the maintenance department. Industries cannot prepare clear budgets for repair, since we do not know how many machines or vehicles will break down and will have to be repaired.

We could try to prepare some kind of preventive repair budget. Management knows how many workers they have for repair activities and has information about this department's operating costs. There may also be historical data of different repairs realized during previous years which could be used to project necessary budget amounts. In any case, in Class 5 we have to open within the repair group of accounts, some Main accounts which relate to repair on buildings, machines, vehicles, office equipment, etc. In addition, some managers need to know repair costs of special equipment; consequently, we will have to open Sub-accounts for these items.

Some direct costs can be identified in the case of repairs, such as parts and supplies, that are requested for specific work.

The store's withdrawals would be credited in Class 2 and allocated directly to the repair accounts in Class 5. Then the corresponding absorption of the departmental operating costs can take place. We would have to prepare some absorption rates for the different repair activities that the industry has to realize.

Those repairs that must be controlled should have their specific Job orders. Once the repair is finished, the total amount of this repair could be handled in either of the following ways:

1. If the amount is relatively small, reallocate this value to the corresponding department in Class 3.

2. If the amount is relatively large, amortize or depreciate it during some time period. This decision should be made by the Financial and Production Cost department.

The reality of having repairs during some months raises the following problem: If a repair were performed during the month of May, we probably will charge this larger or smaller amount to the production of the month of June and subsequent months. This will make the production of these months more expensive, and the unit cost will go up. The question now is, "Is it correct to 'punish' the production that follows the month of repair with this new cost?" Probably not!

But how could we charge some future repair cost to the production that was realized before this repair happened?

There are many different solutions to this problem, but the best solution, in our opinion, is the "internal lease" agreement.

This procedure will be discussed in Chapter 17.

Repair activities in some cases cause quite a problem. Let us here examine the following example situation.

A company has a spare electric motor for an important machine. The motor in the machine breaks down. The repair crew replaces the broken motor with the new one, and takes the old unit for repair to their department. A Job order for this repair is established. After a few days, the motor is repaired and is transferred to the spare parts inventory store. The electric motor will stay in the inventory store until the repair crew needs it to replace another broken unit. Now the issues are:

1. How should we handle the depreciation of the second motor that the company had as a spare unit?

2. How should we amortize the repair cost of the first motor?

When a company purchases expensive spare parts, the production cost should also be charged with the depreciation of this spare part. Should the depreciation of the electric motor correspond to the time period of the depreciation of the principal machine?

It may be that the spare motor never will be used.

The inventory account of spare parts shows the purchase value of the second motor. The first motor is included in the total value of the machine; it is part of the Fixed Assets. How should the requisition of the second motor be recorded? Reduce the value of the inventory and increase the Fixed Assets? Our accounting colleagues will give us the answers.

INTERNAL CONSTRUCTION COSTS

In this chapter, we will discuss the questions related to the control of internal construction. Within this Group of accounts, we have to open several Main accounts for the control of internal production of tools, machines, buildings, etc. And each of these Main accounts may have some Sub-accounts where management is able to identify the construction cost of some specific item, according to need.

The control possibility of internal construction works is especially interesting. Let us look at the following example:

The construction itself will be identified with the Main account of 5740000. This Main account can be divided into 9 different Main accounts organized under the first digit of 40. So, Main account 41 refers to some basic construction work that identifies this project, let us say excavations for the construction. Within this last Main account we may open Sub-accounts to record the different excavation jobs which must be completed. The whole structure looks like this:

5	7	00	000	CONSTRUCTIONS AND PROJECTS
5	7	40	000	CONSTRUCTION # 4
5	7	41	000	EXCAVATIONS
5	7	41	010	Main building # 1
5	7	41	011	Consulting work
5	7	41	012	Engineering tasks
5	7	41	013	Machine lease

This code structure allows for a sophisticated and detailed development, and we may open as many accounts as are necessary and justifiable.

CHAPTER 17

THE MACHINE LEASE AGREEMENT

The whole complex issue of repair costs is very difficult to define, isolate, and control. One reason for this is that it is so easy to start in some random month to charge to production some repair cost that was not anticipated months before. Sometimes it is impossible to know several months ahead that there will be some repair costs for a specific machine. Therefore, no repair charge was allocated over the whole year and subsequently charged to production for the whole year.

A repair problem could also mean that the production for a specific month of the year might be more expensive because repair work had to be realized during this month.

It would seem more appropriate to try, from the beginning of a year, to establish the total operating cost of a machine for a known period. For accountability purposes, it may even be appropriate to calculate the total operating cost of the machine per hour of operation. Once this cost is established, it could be used to determine operating cost for some type of internal lease arrangement that could be used for this machine's production.

The following would be the points of analysis for this project.

1. Establish total operating cost of a machine for a specific time period. If possible this time period should be reduced to one hour.

2. The total operating cost of a machine is to be used as an hourly lease of this machine toward the production activity. This means that production would be charged with the lease cost per hour of using the machine. The same idea applies as if the machine were leased from outside that company.

3. Control the actual operating cost, with the lease cost charged to the production activity, and adjust the lease cost when necessary.

MACHINE OPERATING COSTS

Machine operating cost is the first analysis we need to establish. What are the operating costs of a machine which we would like to control under this "internal lease agreement"? This project would not refer to all machines that we have in our company, but only those that are of interest to this type of control identification.

The following list will help to determine some machine operating costs:

Machine A:	Total purchase price
	Projected operating time: month, hours.
Operating cost per hour:	
	Electric power or fuel
	Depreciation
	Installation space rent
	Maintenance and repair
	Insurance
	Interest cost of capital invested
	Other identifiable costs.

We identified six items to include in this cost, but it could be any number. It is necessary, then, to project maintenance of Machine A during all years and then reduce this amount to refer to one hour of work.

In the same way, we have to budget the repair cost for the entire period this machine is operating and then reduce this cost to one hour of operation. Naturally, the cost is a budgeted cost, that is, it is our projection for future operating costs. Direct Labor force is not included in this table, because it is charged separately.

This will be the operating cost of this machine per hour of work. Any Job order that will use this machine for one hour would be charged with this operating cost per hour.

LEASE OPERATING TRANSACTIONS

Internal lease projects can only be recorded if we have set up a separate Internal Accounting procedure. Therefore, all lease transactions will be recorded in the Internal Accounting.

In Class 2: COST ELEMENTS, we have to open accounts that refer to the Internal Lease Costs. These accounts are to be located within the Group of Depreciation, and a specific Main account serves for that group of machines we wish to control. We may open some Sub-accounts to control specific machines. These accounts have to be credited with the lease amount that will be charged to the Job order of a specific Production Cost account in Class 5. Every time a machine is used for some job, we establish the lease value and credit this amount to the Class 2 account and transfer it to Production cost.

This is a very simple accounting procedure. Graphically, it is done in the following way shown in Exhibit 17-1.

Emanuel Schwarz

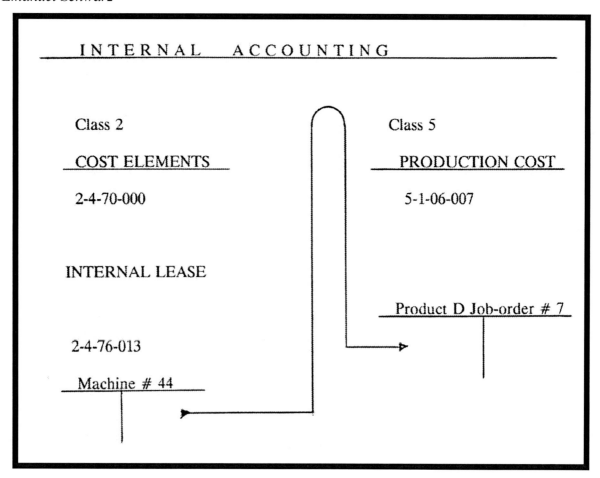

EXHIBIT 17-1: Cost of Lease Transactions.

LEASE OPERATING COST CONTROL

As mentioned before, we have to control the machine operating lease amounts with the actual operating cost of these machines. This is done by opening accounts that show management the actual operating costs of these units and which give information about the variances that occurred during the preceding year. It would not be adequate to analyze <u>monthly</u> variances because the hourly lease cost was calculated to reflect the total repair cost for the year. We establish this lease operating cost per hour for one year and keep this cost without any change. Only under special circumstances is this lease cost per hour to be changed. Management would receive information about such change of lease costs. At the end of the year, we compare the total actual operating cost of the machine(s) with the accumulated lease amount. The variance must be analyzed.

It is possible, for example, that in the first year the lease cost was higher than the actual cost because actual repair cost was very low. It is also possible that the contrary situation may happen at the end of the life time of the machine. There may also be a variance because our budget referred to more or fewer operating hours than the actual happened to be. Whatever the variance, we will need to compare the actual payment for the different items with the budgeted cost for the items. Based upon this analysis, we adjust the operating lease cost for the new budget period of one year.

For proper accounting information, we need to open the following accounts:

1.Class 2: All different Cost Element accounts for fuel/electricity consumption, depreciation, insurance, and interest cost for the item to be controlled.

2.Class 3: Accounts to control maintenance and repair department's operating costs, as we discussed in the previous chapter.

3.Class 5: In Group 3 & 4, accounts to register the actual costs for maintenance and repairs. These accounts would be detailed as management developed the lease control structure. In other words, we would have in this Group of Class 5 the same quantity of accounts as we have established in Class 2, Internal Lease Cost. And to these accounts we will charge the actual maintenance or repair cost.

Every month, we would have the lease amounts in Class 2, and the actual operating costs for these machines that we decided to control in Class 5. At the end of each month, we would have to transfer these amounts to some type of summary accounts in Class 7. It would be adequate to use Group 6, 7, or 8 in Class 7. The balance amounts from Class 2 would be transferred to credit in Class 7 and the amounts accumulated in Class 5 would be transferred to Class 7 via Class 6.

These accounts in Class 7 provide monthly information and their balances will be taken to the Adjusted Operating Profit account in Class 9. At the end of each year, we then have

accumulated amounts of the actual and leased amounts in Class 7 and can analyze them in detail.

Let us look at a graphic presentation of this concept in Exhibit 17-2.

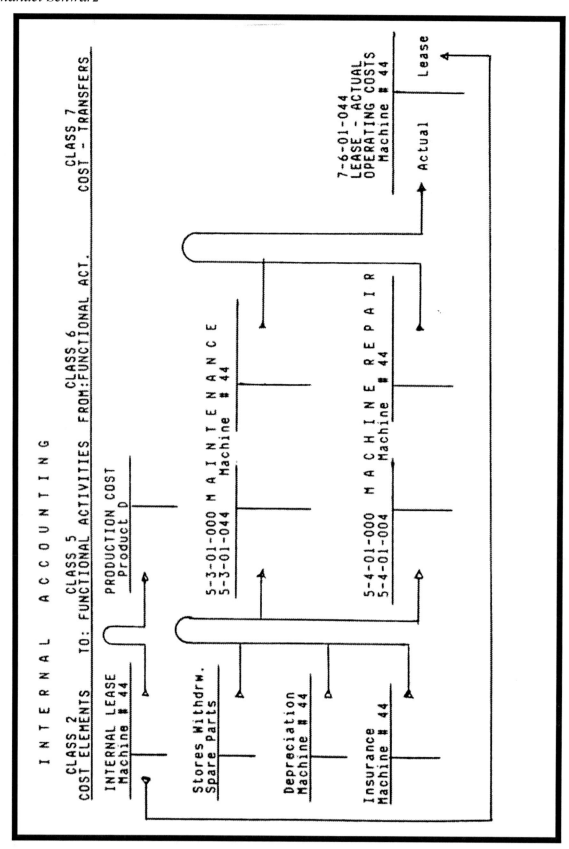

EXHIBIT 17-2: Internal Lease Transactions

CHAPTER 18

TRANSFER ACCOUNTS

Class 7 is a special class of accounts in which we not only have important accounts referring to Cost of Goods Sold, but also Inventory accounts and other Groups of accounts that could be classified as Contra Accounts to some Assets.

One of the basic rules for Internal Accounting is to keep the double entry procedure within the Internal structure. That is, we are not to credit some account in Internal Accounting and carry the debit to some account in the External because we need these inventory accounts to keep entries within the Internal Accounting. These inventory accounts are used as the so-called Contra Accounts, up to the moment when we proceed with month-end closing. In the same way, we also structured the Major Repair and Construction accounts within Group 6 of this Class 7.

Let us now analyze the last of these Contra Accounts in this Class. We refer to them as TRANSFER accounts.

An example helps to understand the need for these transfer accounts.

A company has a branch office where it sells its products. Management likes to keep finished goods inventory control in separate accounts for this branch office. When products are sent to this branch office, we proceed in the following way:

1.Shipment will be credited to Finished Goods Inventory withdrawal account in Class 2 and debited to the corresponding transfer account in Class 7, Group 8. We may call this account Finished Goods transfer to branch office: 7851011.

2.Month-end transaction will take this amount from credit 7851011 to debit Finished Goods Inventory in branch office, which will be an Asset account.

3.Separate documentation will be used to record the financial transactions, which will only refer to the External Accounting.

The same situation may develop if employees have the right to purchase finished goods from the company. The above mentioned first step would be nearly the same with the exception that in Class 7 we have to use some other Main account: Transfer to Employees account.

Exhibit 18-1 illustrates these transactions clearly.

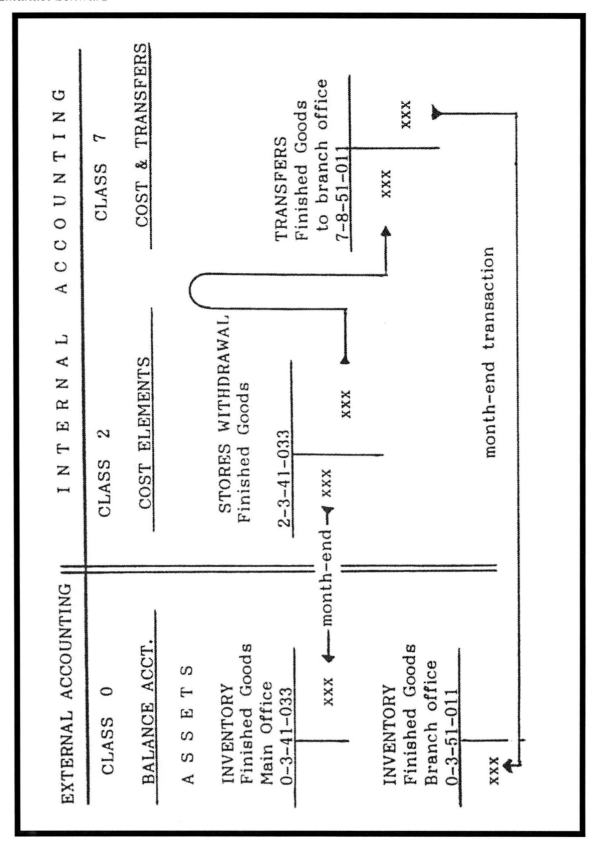

EXHIBIT 18-1: Internal Transfers.

CHAPTER 19

MONTH END CLOSING

Once all the transactions have been realized for a specific accounting period, it is necessary to proceed with the monthly closing of each account. The same basic rules used in Financial Accounting are also used in this Integrated Accounting, which means that only the Balance accounts may have some beginning and ending balance. All other accounts are working accounts. This means they have to show the amount of some Expenditure or Cost for this specific time period for one month; month-end transactions will have to balance these accounts in such a way that no amount will be transferred to the next month. In other words, the working accounts of Class 1 through 8 must send their balances to some other account to prepare the company's Income Statement and to accounts designed to receive the month-end balances.

The Integrated Accounting system starts its month-end closing with the accounts of Class 1, then proceeds to accounts of Class 2, and continues with

Class 3 through 8 using the following month-end closing rules:

CLASS 1:The whole idea of matching costs to the corresponding revenues of the month is represented in Class 1 and 2 accounts and the final variance account. We will discuss this point later.

In Class 1, we also have Non-Operating Expenditure accounts whose balance will have to be transferred at the end of each month to specific accounts in Class 9.

This account is in Class 9, Group 3.

It is better that, in our monthly result analysis, we separate these non-operating expenditures from the operating ones. In this way, we can proceed in Class 9 with the Non-Operating Revenues.

All other accounts within Class 1 take their balances to the Asset accounts.

Recall that these accounts were classified as Contra Accounts. This month-end closing procedure will also be used to prepare reports.

Class 1 will serve as a very important information source about the actual accrued expenditures of the month, and should be compared to the budgeted amounts.

This system of reporting is a guidance to management about actual expenditures compared to the budgeted ones.

CLASS 2: The same rules that apply in Class 1 apply in this Class of the Cost

Elements. Most accounts transfer their balance from debit Class 2 to credit Class 9, Group 4, which is the variance account between Expenditures and Costs.

Special treatment is required with the depreciation account which will have to transfer their balance to a special account in Class 9, Group 2.

The purpose of creating this special account is to give management separate information about the depreciation amounts in our Internal and External accounting.

Let us remember that in Class 2, we do not have Group 9, Non-Operating Expenditure account, as was created in Class 1.

Graphically, we see that Group 9 accounts are outside the frame of the Internal Accounting structure.

Stores Withdrawal in Class 2, will transfer its balance to its "Mother" account in Class 0.

CLASS 3: All accounts in Class 3 will have their balances transferred at the end of the month to a special account in Class 9, Group 5. The Class 9 account will show the variances between the actual departmental operating costs and the absorbed amounts that were recorded in Class 4.

We may create separate variances of over or under absorbed amounts of the different departments within our company. We may possibly need Sub-accounts.

CLASS 4: This class is a counterpart of Class 3; therefore it is obvious that month end closing transactions occur in the same way as in Class 3.

We call to your attention the possibility, however, that in Class 4 we may have fewer accounts than we have in Class 3.

This possibility is shown in the Group 1, Administrative and Sales Departments.

In Class 3 it is preferable to have specific accounts for each department, but in

Class 4 we may open just one account, which will be used to transfer the total absorbed amount from these departments to the Cost of Goods Sold.

Or, we may open just two accounts in Class 4: one for the absorbed administrative costs, and the other for the sales costs.

This procedure is not recommended for such departments as Direct Production , obviously, as we need to know the over or under absorbed amounts of each department.

CLASS 5: As we have learned, these Production Cost accounts must transfer their month-end balance amounts to the Work-in-Process account in Assets.

Consequently, all accounts in Class 5 will take their balance to the Class 0, Group4.

In this Integrated Accounting, we propose to have a group of accounts within Assets, called OTHER ASSETS. But the creation of this group is a matter of preference.

CLASS 6: As these accounts correspond to the Good Output of production, that is, production transferred to Finished Goods Inventory during the month, we have to move the balance amounts to the Work-in-Process accounts in Class 0.

It was previously established that the Work-in-Process account would have several Main accounts and Sub-accounts for better identification of the different amounts in process.

There are two basic Class 7 rules:

1. Any account that corresponds to Cost of Goods Sold will have its balances transferred to the Calculated Operating Profit account in Class 9, Group 7. These costs are to be compared with the revenues received from sales activities.

The Calculated Operating Profit account in Class9 will correspond to an Income Summary account. This Income account is very important, and we will analyze it later in this chapter.

2.   All other Class 7 accounts will have their balances transferred to some Asset accounts. These are so-called Contra accounts to the Assets in Class 7 that are used to hold amounts prior to their period end transfer to a corresponding balance account.

Reports to management referring to these accounts are quite interesting and should be compared monthly to the budgeted values.

CLASS 8 :All balances will be transferred to Class 9 to establish the period result analysis. Those accounts referring to the Sales Revenues must be taken to the 97 account to be compared with the Class7 Cost of Goods Sold amounts.

The balance of the Other Revenues accounts will be taken to the Adjusted Operating Profit account in Class 9.

We would definitely not recommend mixing Sales Revenues with Other Revenues.

Finally, we have accounts that refer to the Non-Operating Revenues in Class 8.

In the Integrated Accounting System, it is preferable to compare these revenues with Non-Operating Expenditure from Class 1. A special group has been reserved for this purpose: Class 9, Group 3.   The amounts of the Non-Operating Revenues are also interesting and worthwhile to analyze.

CLASS 9: SPECIAL RUES

Class 9 is a very important class from which management receives its monthly information along with details about the progress and development of the company.   Here are a variety of accounts in Class 9 which will show the different variances that have occurred during a specific period in the company.

The whole idea of having a special class of accounts for result analysis is very practical for managerial reporting purposes, and we feel that this structure is much more useful for reporting compared with what we have today in the form of the Income Statement.

Class 9 is broadly developed so that it can be used and structured in different ways to satisfy the precise needs of management.

Let us now analyze the different groups of accounts on which the standard structure of the Integrated Accounting System is based:

Group 1: This group is opened to show management different types of variances.

We may use it to analyze the Standard Cost variances such as price variance, etc. As shown in the Exhibit 11-1, the amounts that are charged and credited to this account come from Class 0 accounts.

This is just an example.

These balance amounts may come from any class of accounts.

The graphic layout demonstrates that the balance from this account may be a debit balance or a credit balance. Therefore, the dotted line that goes out of this account is shown leaving the circle's lower , central part. If we follow this dotted line downward, we enter the account identified as 98, Adjusted Operating Profit.

The variances will change the Calculated Operating Profit.

Recall here that the calculated profit is developed with standard costs.

Group 2: This group is specifically used to establish the depreciation variances.

Depreciation that is used in External Accounting is transferred to this account; the Internal depreciation will come from Class 2. We can observe that the balance line that leaves this code 92 account moves downward to the 98 account.

Here we use the same procedure as in Group 1 of this Class, which means that the variance between depreciation of the External accounting and the Internal will have to change the Calculated Operating Profit.

Group 3: This group will show management the Expenditures and Revenues that do

 not correspond to normal activity of the company, the so called non-operating ones. It is useful to have this special group of accounts to give information that should be clearly understood and analyzed by management.

Group 4: This is an important group of accounts because here we demonstrate the whole idea of matching expenditures to revenues.

From Class 1, we debit all Expenditures to Group 4;

from Class 2, all Cost Elements are credited to this same account.

Because we have separated External from Internal Accounting, we now charge (to Class 1) the total amount of expenditures that accrued during this month. We actually do not need to use the Prepaid Expense accounts in Assets, as we today are obliged to do for the purpose of matching the expense with the revenues. Regarding Class 1 accounts, the actual amount is charged to them and then use Class 2 accounts to transfer to the production cost, the corresponding expired portion of the expenditure.

Clearly, the matching problem is not only related with Expense and Revenues, but just as important, is to match the expense with production costs.

The variance between Expenditures and Costs will have to be transferred to the 9 8 account.

Group 5: In this Group we will show the difference between the actual

departmental operating costs and the absorbed amounts charged to production. Management receives all detailed information about over or under absorbed variances. Such information not only refers to the Direct Production Departments, but also to Administrative and Sales Departments, to Indirect Production, and to Service Departments. In these reports the actual operating costs should be compared with the budgeted values.

Group 6: This group is not used in the standard version of the Integrated Accounting System.

Group 7: Group 7 shows the Calculated Operating Profit as it compares the Cost of Goods Sold with the corresponding Revenues. As the debit amounts are transferred from Class 7, and from Class 8 we receive the credit amounts.

Remember that the Cost of Goods Sold should be expressed in standard values, but it is not a must. The profit is a calculated amount.

Group 8: The Calculated Operating Profit will have to be adjusted with the variances between actual and calculated amounts that we have had in the company. This new, Adjusted Operating Profit still refers to normal business activities.

Non-operating values are NOT included.

Group 9: This Group will show the profit or loss that a company has as it corresponds to the Income statement prepared in accordance to the Financial Accounting. In the graphic presentation of Class 9, we can see that the Non Operating Expenditures and Revenues are transferred to this account.

CHAPTER 20

OPERATING PROFITS

The new Integrated Accounting System provides not just one Income Statement, but a whole, logical structure of three different and meaningful Income Statements. Here are the basic concepts of how the system works:

1. 1t is essential to work with Standard Cost within the Internal Accounting System. This will produce a standard cost for finished goods as well as a standard cost for goods sold. As it is set up, this system allows for a strict comparison of revenues with cost of goods sold. Thus, the first income statement will show a calculated standard profit. Still, the system does not oblige the user to work with standard costs; any one of the many different procedures may be used.

All necessary and correctly calculated costs are identified and recorded in Class 7 as Cost of Goods Sold. This is important because these costs fulfill the matching requirements toward revenues. Having the Internal Accounting separated from the External Accounting, we have much more flexibility to properly realize this matching work, not only for the production costs, but also for the administrative and sales operating costs.

Based upon adequate, established costs, this calculated profit should be correct from both an accounting point of view and an economic business point of view. Working with standard costs, the calculated profit will be the same every month if the sales volume, expressed in units, stays at the same level. If such calculated profit under the abovementioned conditions is different from that of the month before, the reason for such a change must proceed from the sales activity. The company simply may have not sold at the same sales price.

Let us clarify an important point:

> WE ARE NOT REFERRING TO THE TOTAL COST OF GOODS SOLD
> AND TOTAL REVENUES, WE REFER TO A SPECIFIC PRODUCT.

In this Calculated Operating Profit account, we are able to compare the revenues of a specific product with its corresponding cost of goods sold. This detailed information is recorded in some Sub-accounts. In Main accounts, we have the accumulated information for a group of products; In the Group account, we have the total calculated operating profit for the company.

This calculated profit is important for such conditions as paying managerial sales commissions based upon profit. Having calculated values, we are able to pay the same amounts of commission independently, if production shows positive or negative efficiency or price variance.

For internal managerial information, this calculated profit would be the most important one, as it reflects the sales efficiency of the company. The next important point is the information about variances that the company had in its purchase activity, production process, administrative, and sales activities. These details are accumulated in the Adjusted Operating Profit account.

2. The account 98 refers to the Adjusted Operating Profit.

    The Calculated Profit/Loss from account 97 is transferred to this new account, Adjusted Operating Profit account. Here we have to add or subtract variances that have their origin in comparing actual costs to standard costs.

    Let us, for example, analyze raw material variances:

    Price variance for raw material withdrawn from inventory can be tracked to specific Job orders. Knowing these Job orders, we can also know the product that was produced. However, it would not be possible to follow this Job order to sales since the finished goods inventory is not controlled by Job orders. The same finding also corresponds to Efficiency variances.

    The point is that raw material variances be verified and analyzed in the process of production by each Job order, and not just when the product is sold. These same determinations are also related to Direct Labor Wage variances and to the over or under absorption variances. The whole point of having a 98 Group is to change the Calculated Operating Profit to the amount needed in our Financial Accounting. The difference is that this adjusted profit has no amounts which do not correspond to our normal operating activities.

3. The Integrated Accounting System develops the Income Statement, which corresponds to the External Accounting and is completed for tax payment purposes. Adjusted Operating Profit is regulated with the non-operating expenditures and revenues, resulting in Class 9, Group 9 the taxable profit of the company.

We may say that the final bottom line figure, the taxable profit, is a consequence of a clear, accurate, complete and meaningful development of a managerial cost system.

Emanuel Schwarz

REFERENCES

Anderson, Henry R., Belverder E. Needles, J.Caldwell
MANAGERIAL ACCOUNTING
Houghton Mifflin Company, 1989.

Anthony, Robert N., Glenn A. Welsch, James Reece
FUNDAMENTALS OF MANAGEMENT ACCOUNTING
Richard D. Irwin, Inc. 4th Edition, 1985.

Anthony, Robert N., John Dearden
MANAGEMENT CONTROL SYSTEM
Richard D. Irwin, Inc., 4th Edition, 1980.

Cherrington, J. Owen, E. Dee Hubbart, D.H. Luthy
COST AND MANAGERIAL ACCOUNTING
West Publishing Company, 2nd Edition, 1985.

Cooper, Robin and Robert S. Kaplan
HOW COST ACCOUNTING SYSTEMATI. DISTORTS PROD.
Accounting & Management: Harvard Business P.,1987

Cooper, Robin and Robert S. Kaplan
MEASURE COSTS RIGHT, MAKE THE RIGHT DECISIONS
Harvard Business Review, Sept. Oct. 1988.

Davidson, Sidney, Michael W. Maher, C. Stickney
MANAGERIAL ACCOUNTING: AN INTROD.TO CONCEPTS.
The Dryden Press, 3rd. Edition, 1988.

Deakin, Edward B. and Michael W. Maher
COST ACCOUNTING
Irwin, 2nd. Edition, 1987.

Ferrara, William L., Frank Dougherty, Wayne Keller
MANAGERIAL COST ACCOUNTING:PLANNING AND CONTROL
Dame Publications Inc. 1987.

Fess, Philip E. and Carl S. Warren
MANAGERIAL ACCOUNTING
SouthWestern Publishing Co., 1985.

Foster, George and Charles Horngren
JIT:COST ACCOUNTING AND COST MANAGEMENT ISSUES
Management Accounting, June 1987.

Garrison, Ray H.
MANAGERIAL ACCOUNTING: CONCEPTS FOR PLANNING
Business Publications, Inc. 1988.

Gray, Jack and Don Ricketts

COST AND MANAGERIAL ACCOUNTING
McGrawHill Book Company, 1982

Hall, Robert W.
MEASURING PROGRESS: MANAGEMENT ESSENTIAL
Target, Summer 1987.

Hartley, Ronald V.
COST AND MANAGERIAL ACCOUNTING
Allyn and Bacon, Inc. 1983.

Heitger, Lester E. and Serge Matulich
MANAGERIAL ACCOUNTING
McGrawHill Book Company, 2nd Edition, 1986.

Helmkamp, John G.
MANAGERIAL ACCOUNTING
John Wiles & Sons, 1st Edition, 1987.

Hirsch, Maurice L. Jr, and Joseph G. Louderback
COST ACCOUNTING: ACCUMULATION, ANALYSIS AND USE
Kent Publishing Company, 2nd Edition, 1986.

Horngren, Charles T. and Gary L. Sundem
INTRODUCTION TO MANAGEMENT ACCOUNTING
PrenticeHall, Inc. 7th Edition, 1987.

Horngren, Charles T. and George Foster
COST ACCOUNTING A MANAGERIAL EMPHASIS
PrenticeHall, 6th Edition, 1987.

Johnson, H. Thomas
ACTIVITYBASED INFORMATION: A BLUEPRINT
Management Accounting, June 1988.

Johnson, H. Thomas
ORGANIZATIONAL DESIGN VERSUS STRATEGIC INFORM.
Acctg.and Manag.Boston: Harvard B.School P. 1987.

Johnson, H. Thomas and Robert S. Kaplan
RELEVANCE LOST:THE RISE AND FALL OF MANAGEMENT
Harvard Business School Press, 1987.

Johnson, H. Thomas and Dennis A. Loewe
HOW WEYERHAEUSER MANAGES OVERHEAD COSTS
Management Accounting, August 1987.

Kaplan, Robert S.
THE EVOLUTION OF MANAGEMENT ACCOUNTING
Accounting Review, July 1984.

Kaplan, Robert S.
ONE COST SYSTEM ISN'T ENOUGH
Harvard Business Review, Jan.Feb. 1988.

Kaplan, Robert S.
ACCOUNTING LAG: THE OBSOLESCENCE OF COST
California Management Review, Winter 1986.

Kaplan, Robert S.
ADVANCED MANAGEMENT ACCOUNTING
PrenticeHall, Inc. 1982.

Kaplan, Robert S. and Anthony A. Atkinson
ADVANCED MANAGEMENT ACCOUNTING
Prentice Hall, 2nd. Edition, 1989.

Killough, Larry N. and Wayne E. Leininger
COST ACCOUNTING, CONCEPTS/TECHNIQUES
West Publishing Company, 1984.

Liao, Woody M. and James L. Boockholdt
COST ACCOUNTING FOR MANAGERIAL PLANNING
Dame Publications, Inc. 1989.

Matz, Adolph, and Milton F. Usry
COST ACCOUNTING PLANNING AND CONTROL
SouthWestern Publishing Co., 8th Edition, 1984.

Miller, Jeffrey and Thomas Vollman
THE HIDDEN FACTORY
Harvard Business Review, Sept.Oct. 1985.

Moore, Carl L., Lane Anderson, Robert Jaedicke
MANAGERIAL ACCOUNTING
SouthWestern Publishing Co., 1988.

Moriarty, Shane and Carl P. Allen
COST ACCOUNTING
Harper & Row, Publishers, 1984.

Morse, Wayne J., James R. Davis, Al L.Hartgraves
MANAGEMENT ACCOUNTING
AddisonWesley Publishing Company, 2nd Edition, 1988.

Moscove, Stephen A., Gerald Crowningshield, Gorman
COST ACCOUNTING WITH MANAGERIAL APPLICATIONS
Houghton Mifflin Company, 5th Edition, 1985.

Most, Kenneth S., and Ronald J. Lewis
COST ACCOUNTING
Grid Publishing, Inc., 1982

Norgaard, Corine T.
MANAGEMENT ACCOUNTING
Prentice Hall, Inc., 1985.

Rayburn, L. Gayle
PRINCIPLES OF COST ACCOUNTING
Irwin, 4th Edition, 1989.

Schmalenbach, Ernst
DER KONTENRAHMEN
Wirtschaftshochschule von Koeln, 1927.

Shillinglaw, Gordon
MANAGERIAL COST ACCOUNTING
Richard D. Irwin, Inc., 1977.

Shillinglaw, Gordon and Philip E. Meyer
ACCOUNTING: A MANAGEMENT APPROACH
Irwin, 8th Edition, 1986.

Skare, Leif H. and Nils Vaesthagen
INDUSTRIELL SJALVKOSTNADSBERAKNING
P.A. Norsted, 2nd Edition, Stockholm, 1949.

Usry, Miltion, F., Lawrence H. Hammer, Adolph Matz
COST ACCOUNTING PLANNING AND CONTROL
SouthWestern Publishing Co., 9th Edition, 1988.

Vehn, A. ter
MEKANFORBUNDETS NORMALKONTOPLAN
Sveriges Mekanforbund, Stockholm 1957.

ABOUT THE AUTHOR

The author studied in Sweden, at Stockholm School of Economics, and was hired by the United Nations Industrial Development Organization (UNIDO) in Vienna, Austria as a consultant for Governmental enterprises in South America.

During these 10 years the Author put into practical work the new approach of Internal Accounting.

Since 1979 the Author settled down in San Jose, California with his family, and was called to teach Managerial Accounting at San Francisco State University, in San Francisco.

At present Schwarz is a Professor Emeritus, retired from the university.

Over 12 years Professor Schwarz worked on his research project to develop the Internal Accounting for American industries.

This research project had now been published for over a year in the web site of

Pro2 Net, in Seattle, Washington.

Dr. Schwarz's project has received international attention over the years.

9 780759 631694